My Son Jimi

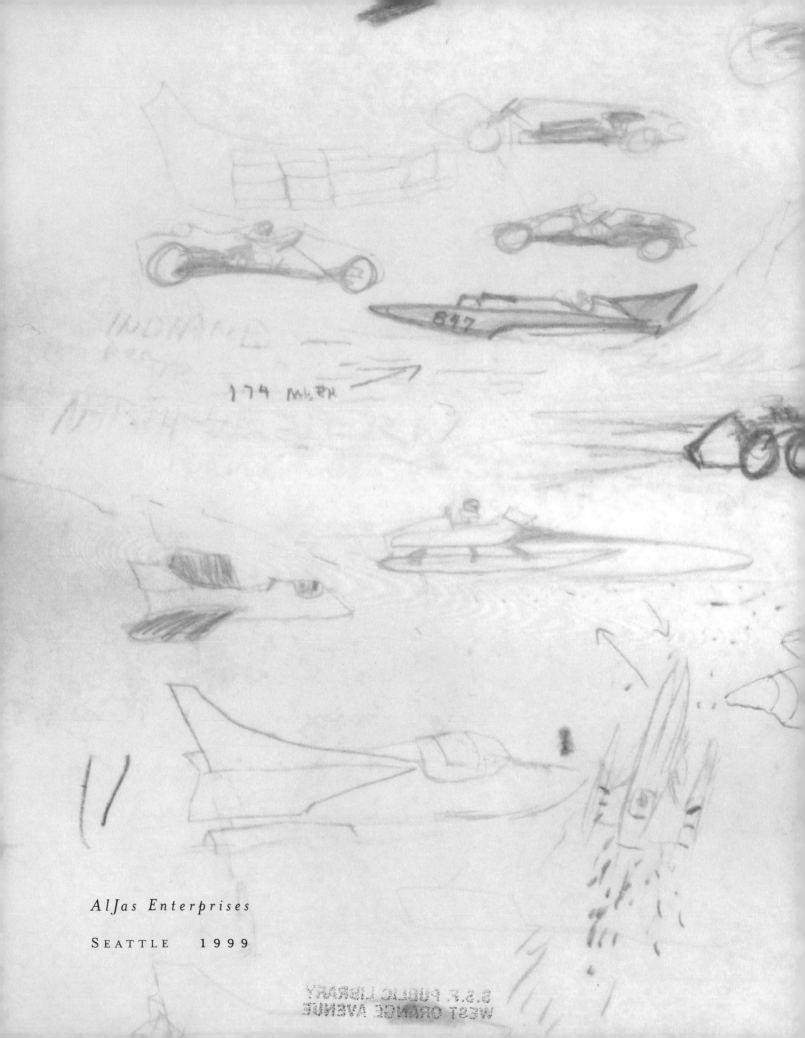

AlJas Enterprises

Seattle   1999

James A. Hendrix

JAIL HOUSE ROCK

My Son Jimi

As told to Jas Obrecht

AlJas Enterprises, L.P.
P.O. Box 88070
Seattle,WA 98138
U.S.A.

ISBN 0-9667857-0-3

JACKET / BOOK DESIGNER
Saroyan Humphrey

First Edition

To the family.

EVER SINCE I helped bring him into this world, I've struggled to do right by my son. I wrote *MY SON JIMI* after winning back Jimi's musical legacy in 1995 because it finally felt like he had come back home. I also wanted to get the story of his life straightened out before something happens to me. So many books about Jimi have come out over the past twenty-five years, and I knew none of them could come off properly because the authors didn't interview me or any of the family all that much,

A Message from G.H.Q.

although some of them said they would. Writers who've never talked with Jimi or me don't know anything about his childhood, and his childhood had a whole lot of bearing on who he became. I just got so tired of seeing so much garbage and made-up stuff, I had to set the record straight.

With this book, I want to let people know what Jimi was all about—where he came from, who his people were, and how we lived while he was growing up. This is his story, and it's coming direct from G.H.Q.— that's General Headquarters.

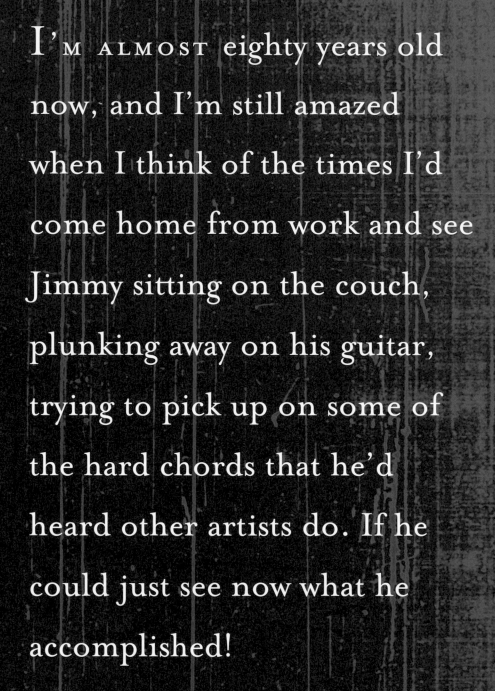

I'M ALMOST eighty years old now, and I'm still amazed when I think of the times I'd come home from work and see Jimmy sitting on the couch, plunking away on his guitar, trying to pick up on some of the hard chords that he'd heard other artists do. If he could just see now what he accomplished!

People are always asking me if Jimmy had a sense of how great he was. I don't think he did.

EVEN WHEN HE WAS FIRST LEARNING TO PLAY GUITAR, JIMMY REALLY GOT INTO IT.

While he was learning guitar, he was saying, "Oh, man, I wish I could play like B.B. King." Maybe he even surpassed him, in a way, but Jimmy himself wouldn't think like that. I know that because sometimes a fan would tell him, "Oh, you're the greatest. You're like an icon."

Jimmy would just say, "Hey, man, get off that stuff. I ain't the greatest. I'm just doing my thing. Don't make me a god—I ain't no god. I got blood running through my veins just like you." He hated to be thought of in any other way.

Ever since Jimmy passed away in 1970, the one thing everybody wants to know is what he was like when he was a kid. They ask me if I saw something special in him, like a halo around him or something of that sort. I always say, "No, he was an ordinary, run-of-the-mill kid coming along, but he had an imagination."

To really understand Jimmy, you have to go back to his beginnings, to that blood running through his veins. Some of Jimmy's ancestors were Indians and slaves. Jimmy was fascinated by his Indian heritage, and my mother used to talk to him about it. Although she never was on

A STUDIO POSTCARD OF MY DAD AND MOM SITTING IN A FAKE CAR.

a reservation, we did have some Indian relics around the house when I was young, like an Indian peace pipe up on the mantel. I'm sure Jimmy saw it while he was growing up. He was always interested in things of that sort.

As a kid, Jimmy liked to dress himself up as much like an Indian as he could, and he and his friends would play cowboys and Indians. Jimmy was interested in his black ancestry as well, but that was somewhat different—no one wanted to play the slave! Having slave ancestors was a common thing among all blacks. It was all in the past, and it was something we just had to live with. Jimmy understood all that.

My mother told me there were slaves on her side of the family and that my dad's mother was a slave. Her name was Fanny, and a slave overseer sired the child who became my father, Bertram Philander Ross Hendrix. I don't know too much about my dad's side of the family. He didn't do much talking about his past or family. I know he had sisters, and my mother told me that he'd been married before. My mother also told me that my dad was from Urbana, Ohio. When I was in

MY MOM, NORA HENDRIX, IN HER SHOWBIZ YEARS.

WHO'S THAT LITTLE FAT DUDE? YOURS TRULY, JAMES ALLEN ROSS HENDRIX.

Mom used to dance with a Dixieland band. My mother's sister called herself
Belle Lamar. That was her stage name.

the service during World War II, a guy told me there were still a lot of Hendrixes living there.

My mother's real name was Zenora, but people called her Nora. She was beautiful—you can see some of Jimmy in her face. She was born in Georgia and raised in Tennessee. She wasn't a Cherokee princess, like some have written, although her grandmother, who was also named Fanny, was a full-blooded Cherokee. The first time I read anything on the subject, it claimed Jimmy's grandmother was part Cherokee. They had that right. I'd tell my mother about that, and she'd just laugh about it. She'd say, "Oh, yeah, that's true."

But they couldn't leave it alone by just saying "part Cherokee." Later on the rumor started that Jimmy's *mother* was Cherokee, and then it became "full-blooded Cherokee." I said, "Oh,

boy. The tale gets more fantastic." After that a lot of people thought it was on his mother's side, and so I finally started telling people, "No, it's on his grandmother's side—on *my* mother's side." And of course they didn't see it that way, but that's where Jimmy's Indian ancestry came from.

My mom's grandfather was English or Irish, and she remembered he'd always be singing these old-style Irish ditties. My mother's parents were named Moore, and they had a farm. Mom enjoyed living there—they had milk and chickens and nearly all the things that

The whole gang. From left, that's my
sister Pat, my brother Leon, me, and my
brother Frank on Richards Street.

12

you'd want—but she and her sister wanted to see the world, so they became entertainers. Her sister went by the stage name of Belle Lamar, and she used to sing and dance and crack jokes. Jimmy knew her when he was small.

My dad and mom were in show business together, but I don't know if that's how they met. Dad was a stagehand, and mom loved to dance. They toured in a company owned by Mr. Cohen, traveling from city to city doing all-black entertainment with skits and a chorus line. It wasn't a minstrel show, but just ordinary black entertainment.

When they came to Seattle around 1911, the show broke up and everybody was out of work. Mr. Cohen told my dad, "I have a friend up in Vancouver, British Columbia. You can go up there and get a job." There wasn't any work around Seattle, so my dad and mom moved up to Vancouver, and he started working as a steward at the Quilchena Golf Club. That was the only job I ever knew him to have.

I was the youngest of their four children. My brother Frank was just eight months older than me, and Leon was the oldest. I gave Jimmy Leon's middle name—Marshall—because I thought a great deal of my oldest brother. I'd tell Jimmy stories about him, because I was so proud of Leon. He'd watch over me. He was very artistic and smart in school, and he graduated from high school. I don't know what year Leon was born, but he was five or six years older than me.

My sister was named Patricia, and we called her Pat. She was born in 1914—that's the beginning of the First World War, and we always associated that with her birth: "That's the reason why the war started—on account of she was born!" My mother used to say, "Yeah, that girl gave me more trouble than those three boys." That's why I always said I'd prefer to have boys.

I was born on June 10, 1919. My full name is James Allen Ross Hendrix. The name Allen was given to me by Mrs. Williams, my godmother. Ross was part of my father's name. Although my first name is James, people have always called me Al or Allen. When I asked my mother why, she told me that our neighbors, the Clarks, had a son named Jimmy, and he and I did a lot of running around together, so they used my second name to keep us separated.

When I was born, our family was living at 2225 Triumph Street in a nice, comfortable little place with a wood-burning stove and bay room with mom's flowerpots in the window. In those days I was around my mother most of the time because my dad was always busy working. He'd leave around seven o'clock in the morning, and we'd all kiss him good-bye. He had to take streetcars all the way out to the golf course, and he wouldn't be home until around seven or eight in the evening. We'd always wait until he'd come home before we'd eat supper.

Mom was kind of ordinary in her dress and manners, while dad was so distinguished he was almost aristocratic. He wore a tie, and I remember him talking about dressing for dinner. I said, "Oh, dad's got to be joking! The rich big folks do that." We'd hear about that in the theater pictures, and it seemed like a whole lot of uppity-uppity. Dad wasn't a stuffed shirt, but he wanted to be right and proper, like my brother Frank, who took right after him in that respect. Frank was one for having things just right. He'd spend more time in the bathroom than a woman, getting every little hair to lay down just right. He shined his shoes so much the kids would ask, "Do you put shellac on your shoes? You can see your face in them." Mom could dress up when she got a notion to, but ordinarily she just liked to go casual.

My dad was stern but patient, and he was

MY DAD WAY BACK IN THE DAYS OF CARRIAGES.

real quiet. He was congenial—he'd laugh and talk—but he always held himself real proper. He didn't play around with his kids much, although I remember him reading the comics to me while I was sitting on his lap. He never did give me any whippings, but I was the only one that didn't get a little licking on the butt. But I had a conscience, and when I misbehaved my mother would sit and talk to me and hurt my feelings, and I'd cry on account of her. I'd tell her, "Why don't you just give me a paddling?"

"No!" she'd always say.

Mom called me "Allie," and she was very affectionate with me. I got my sensitivity from her, and probably my sense of humor too. She'd kid around and carry on with the best of them. She was crazy about jokes. She liked to listen to Jack Benny on the radio. Another one of her favorite comedians was Moms Mabley. Jimmy had a sense of humor similar to hers, and the three of us all liked to joke and clown and tease in a natural way. Jimmy was always on the shy side, but he wasn't a wallflower. He liked to clown and carry on and romp with his friends. I could see a lot of similarities between my mother and Jimmy, like in certain little things they'd do or say. Some of the things I do myself remind me of my mother, and I have to laugh about that sometimes.

Frank and I played together a lot with the kids in the neighborhood. We liked to play cowboys and Indians, running around shooting at each other. I was always the Indian! We didn't have a whole lot of toys, so we'd get into my mother's clothespin bag and make a bunch of soldiers and have them all lined up and battling each other. We got the idea from

Leon, who used to make little cars out of cardboard—he'd dress up the cars and have them on display around the house.

My dad didn't play golf, but sometimes the members would throw clubs and balls away, and my dad would bring them home. Leon built a little five-hole putt-putt course out in the back yard, with tin cans in the ground for the holes. Every Sunday we'd go out there and putt around in the yard, but I didn't start playing golf seriously until after I came out of the service.

My sister Pat and I didn't get along when we were kids. While we were still living on Triumph Street, they had the Canadian Exposition at Hastings Park every year. My mother worked out there sometimes, and she'd take me around to go on different rides. I used to love the ponies. One time mom had to work, so she said, "Pat can take you around." But Pat didn't want to take me, and I didn't feel like going with her because I knew there'd be no fun there. Sure enough, I wanted to ride one of the live ponies, but she wouldn't go for that. I said, "How about the merry-go-round?"

"Okay."

I wanted to get on one of the wooden horses, but she said no and sat me down on one of the ordinary seats. That's the way it was with Pat. There wasn't any use in asking—she'd just say no. She was stricter than my mom, and I stayed clear of her. Some brothers and sisters don't get along.

While we lived on Triumph Street, I went to the Hastings grade school. My brother Frank, who was one grade ahead of me, was always cool-looking. The gals would fall all over him. He didn't have to say anything. He'd just sit there and they'd say, "Ooh, who's that gorgeous man?" Me, I had to do a whole lot of talking. A lot of people said Frank took after my mother, who was fair-skinned. Dad was dark, like my sister Pat, but he had sharp features. My mother looked more Negroid.

Frank had my mother's light skin complexion and my dad's features.

Some of the kids thought Frank was white, which caused some funny situations after we moved on Davie Street in what's now downtown Vancouver. Frank and I started going to Dawson School, and the teachers wanted to know all the kids' phone numbers. I couldn't remember ours, so I told the teacher that I had a brother in one of the classrooms, and she told me to get the number from him. I went to Frank's classroom. He was the only black in there, but they didn't know that. The teacher let me in the door, and I said, "I come to see my brother," and explained to her what I was there for.

She looked around and said, "Where's your brother?"

I walked up to Frank to get the phone number, and everybody looked like, "Huh? Wow!" I don't know how that affected Frank, because he never mentioned it again.

Our house on Davie was right on the alley, and across the street from us was a hotel with a beer parlor on the main floor. One day Frank and I were running around playing with a white kid while my mother was standing on the porch. One of the guys coming out from the beer parlor was a little tipsy, and he gave some change to my mother and said, "Give this to the little colored kid over there."

She said, "Ooh, which one?"

"The little colored kid!"

So my mother started giving some to Frank and some to me too. The guy said, "No, no, not that kid"—he was talking about Frank—"I mean the little colored kid."

My mother just looked at him and said, "He's colored too!" She always laughed about that. But when people would meet Frank and learn he was my brother, they'd usually do a double take.

Looking the way I did, I learned about prejudice when I was young. People just wanted to insult me sometimes. I'd be minding my own business, going down the street, and some white men would come along and say, "Hey, Sambo," or "Hey, Rastus." I couldn't do anything about it because they were a whole lot bigger than me, but I'd tell them, "You wouldn't be saying that if I was your size or if I was my older brother or dad!"

They'd say, "Don't be smart with me!"

Actually, my older brother Leon wasn't a fighter. Jimmy took after him in that way, and he was built like him too—very tall and slim. Like Leon, Jimmy didn't go in for a whole lot of fighting, but he'd stand up for himself. He didn't pick fights or go around bullying people—none of us ever did any of that—but we stood up for our rights.

Sometimes Frank and I had disagreements, and we'd tussle around. Some of the kids rooted for me and some rooted for Frank. But we never did throw a punch at each other. We'd just roll around on the floor and then we'd get up and look at each other and start laughing. To us, it seemed crazy for brothers to be fighting and punching. But I did like to box.

MY MOTHER'S FRIEND PAT WITH
FRANK, ME, AND BERNICE
AT 1343 RICHARDS STREET.

Some of the kids had boxing gloves, and we'd get out in the yard and bang each other around. I just liked the sport. It was almost like fencing, only with your hands. I never fought for real, though, unless provoked. When they started calling me a name, then I'd bang them in their chops real quick.

We went to the movies a lot back then, and my parents went to live shows too. I saw some minstrel performers with them. My mother was always asking my dad if they could go out dancing. Dad belonged to the Elks Club and my brother Frank and I belonged to the Junior Elks, but even when the Elks put on a function, my father never did dance. My mother always said he didn't know how to. He'd just walk around and gab with the guys while my mother was out there dancing with a partner. My dad was quite a bit older than my mother—twenty years or something like that—and he walked with a cane. He had trouble with his feet or legs. My dad didn't drink, either, but my mother did. She made her own dandelion wine in a big crock in the kitchen. Everybody was aware of Prohibition in the United States, and we knew a whole lot of people who were bootlegging. Heck, there was nothing to making wine.

We used to have picnics. The church or Elks Club would have them, or we'd go out with a few friends and have a barbecue at Belcarra Park, Borne Island, or the old Stanley Park—nearly everybody in Vancouver went there. We

THAT'S MY DAD STANDING BY A CAR, ALTHOUGH WE NEVER OWNED ONE.

also went to Kitsilano Beach and had a lot of picnics at Indian Reserve. The water wasn't far from our house, so I did a lot of saltwater fishing too, just dropping in a line with hooks and a weight. As a boy, Jimmy liked to fish like that too.

Eventually my family moved to a big old house at 1343 Richards Street, over on Vancouver's West Side. My dad wanted to get something bigger, and this place had a full basement and a larger front yard and back yard. Our house became a central spot for all the kids in the neighborhood. Frank and I got into making wooden guns there. Frank would get pictures from books, and we'd cut guns out of wood and put cylinders on them. We made rifles too—bolt-action army rifles and the Winchester type. We were good at making things like that. One time us kids even built a house on stilts out in the back.

I got to be everyday buddies with Harry Hastings, who was Scotch, and Maso Ono, who was Japanese. Frank was friends with them too. We all used to play cricket together. I was a pretty good pitcher—I'd wind up and put that old Yorker ball on them. We made our own bats, because we didn't have any way of buying one. You'd have a hard time finding any cricket bats anyway, because not too many Canadians played cricket. Harry, Maso, and I did a lot of running around together, and we

stayed friends.

My family belonged to the A.M.E. Church—that's African Methodist. I went to the Sunday school sessions every week, and they taught us about the bible, Jesus Christ, and God. The Sunday school teacher would read some scriptures, give us something to study over the week, and then she'd get back to it the following Sunday and ask questions. My mom and dad didn't go to church every week, because Sunday was often my dad's only day off from work. A lot of times he'd work Sunday too, but if he happened to get home early, sometimes he'd take the whole family to church in the evening. They sang so many songs at church—"Oh, My Good Lord, Show Me the Way," "Swing Low, Sweet Chariot," "Rock of Ages."

DAD ALWAYS LOOKED OVER THE NEWSPAPER. HE LIKED THE *Vancouver Sun*.

❧   ❧   ❧

JIMMY'S MUSICAL aptitude probably came from our side of the family. When I was growing up, we were around music all the time. We'd listen to it on the radio. Around Christmastime we listened to choirs singing carols at department stores. We sang spirituals in the house, like "Swing Low, Sweet Chariot." We did that a lot. I'd be sitting there in the kitchen while my mother would be ironing, and she'd strike up and start singing a song. Maybe my sister would harp in, and pretty soon we'd all do our own little bit. It was a

LEON AND BERNICE. MY OLDEST BROTHER HAD HANDS JUST LIKE JIMMY'S.

family entertainment.

My dad sang with a jubilee choir—that was the only entertainment I ever saw him do. I don't even know if he was a baritone or tenor, because I never did hear him sing around the house. He only sang in a group, and I'd go see him. The music director took the whole choir around to different places to sing.

It was natural that I became a fan of blues music, because we were singing the blues all the time back then! We had a wind-up gramophone and some 78 records of the old stars. One song was about "going to Chicago, darn, but I can't take you." My brother Leon played that all the time on the gramophone. My mother would sing along to it and talk about the blues. She'd say to Leon, "Play 'em that old blues song!" I liked it too. We got to hear so much of that music. I'd sit there and wind up that old gramophone and play Louis Armstrong's "I'll Be Glad When You're Dead, You Rascal You." We also had the "Lone Ranger Theme" and some other classical records. My parents and Leon bought those.

We knew an elderly man, Mr. Simms, who played the guitar. I called him Uncle Joe, and his partner, Mr. Fuller, played the violin. They'd come by every once in a while and play all kinds of different numbers together. We also had a lot of parties on Richards Street, and the elders would play parlor games. They had one game where they'd all get in a circle, and then they'd get a long string and put a ring on it. Everyone in the circle would hold the string and secretly slide the ring from hand to hand while they were singing. One person in the center was supposed to guess who had the ring, only they called it a "thimble." People would sing, "Who's got that thimble," and someone would answer "bangaloo" in a deep bass voice. All the while, they'd be sliding their hands along the string and passing the ring. When the person in the center guessed who had it, then the person who got caught had to get in the center. My brothers, sister, and I would sit on the stairs and watch them have a ball playing this game. Oh, there was a whole lot of rhythm and harmony when they'd get to moving and dancing, and the parts all worked together.

I learned to read music in school. If someone gave me a sheet of music with the notes to a song I'd never heard before, I'd be able to read it and sing at the same time, as long as it didn't have too many of those little sharps and flats. I'd get lost with them, but with just ordinary scales I was okay.

Leon played the violin. He had large hands with long, tapering fingers that were on the delicate side. Jimmy had hands just like his. I have big hands too, but my fingers are just wide. Frank had rather artistic hands too.

We had a piano at home, and my mom could play it somewhat. Leon played the piano too, and he was good because dad got a tutor for him and my sister. Leon could read music, and of course he had his own style too. Leon would play a lot of what we called jazz in those days. He died before the boogie woogie came out, but I used to be able to do a little boogie woogie on the piano. Then after my dad died and we got on welfare, we had to sell the piano, so I lost all touch with playing piano. But I never did get any lessons; I picked it up by watching

I THOUGHT SO MUCH OF MY BROTHER LEON, I GAVE JIMMY HIS MIDDLE NAME—MARSHALL.

my brother and playing by ear.

I was always interested in rhythm. As a little kid, I always thought about being an entertainer or a tap dancer. My family had a hand-me-down tradition from way back when people lived so far apart and traveling was difficult. When friends or relatives would come by to visit, they'd stay there all day long. The parents would tell their kids, "Do something for Mrs. Jones," and you'd recite something or do a little dance or sing a song. So when some of my parents' grown-up friends came by, my mom would say, "C'mon, Al, do a dance." The first dance I ever learned was the Charleston, and so I'd do that and they'd give me some money. Now when Jimmy was coming along, people didn't do all that. He'd be out playing in the dirt with some of his friends when people came over, and I wouldn't have him recite or sing. Jimmy didn't show any signs that he'd become an entertainer until he got that guitar! A lot of the time, though, I'd sing and dance around Jimmy at home, and he'd watch me.

Even when I was little, I'd pick up steps by watching people dance. Frank and Pat could dance too, and Leon did a lot of entertaining. He was smart and popular. A lot of gals were all crazy about him, and he was quite a ladies' man. He had a regular dancing partner, and they'd rehearse at the house and dance for different types of entertainment. They'd tap dance and do the waltz and Spanish dances like the tango. They also did the Apache dance, where the guy tossed the gal all around. Leon and my mother taught me some tap, and my mother taught me to "fall off the log"—a lot of the dancers still do it, but now they put taps into it. She talked about the buck-and-wing and cakewalk. Leon taught me the Charleston and the lindy hop. They had another one called the lazy walk. We teased our sister about that one: "Pat, she can do the lazy walk."

When I was ten or eleven, Pat had a daughter, Grace, who was the only child she ever had. My mother did a lot of taking care of Gracie when she was a baby, naturally, because she was at the house while Pat worked. Frank and I did a lot of baby-sitting too. When she was old enough to talk, Gracie used to call Harry and Maso "Uncle Harry" and "Uncle Maso."

A little neighbor girl named Bernice was around a lot, and we did a lot of baby-sitting for her too. We knew her when she was born. Bernice is in a lot of our family photographs, and she was killed not long after those pictures were taken. They never did figure out how she was poisoned. The couple taking care of her got to accusing each other and broke up after that.

It was devastating because the day before Bernice died, she was following me home from school. I told her, "Quit following me!" There was nothing big about it, but it bothered me afterwards. She lived a couple of blocks up the street from us, and I usually walked right past her house on my way to Dawson School. When I was going to school the next day, Mrs. Elsie McAdoo, Bernice's adoptive mother, hailed me. She told me to tell Bernice's teacher that Bernice had died last night.

I said, "What!?" Because just the day before she was hale and hearty. I went to the princi-

pal's office and told them what she said. They went through a lot of investigations and did an autopsy on Bernice, but they never did find out how she really died.

My sister Pat and Vivian Jones, an old friend of the family.

❦ ❦ ❦

TIMES GOT TOUGH when the Depression came along. We didn't know what an allowance was. Once in a while dad gave me a quarter, but we were running around with just lint in our pockets most of the time.

All the kids used to collect beer bottles and milk bottles and cash them in. Harry Hastings' older brother Huey, who was a lot older than me, taught me to use a magnet to collect aluminum, brass, and copper. I'd go around with him, and we'd collect it, separate it, and take it to the junk guy, who'd weigh it and pay us for it. I also made money stacking wood. Everybody around the neighborhood had wood-sheds, and they'd buy yards of wood to heat their homes and cook their meals. The wood man would just dump it off in the alley, and some people weren't able to bring it in, so I'd do that for them for two bits or fifty cents.

I wanted to find out all the different ways to make money. Shoot, back then you had to hustle around to make your nickels and dimes, but there was a lot less crime. Nobody around the neighborhood ever complained about anybody breaking in. You could go to the grocery store a block away and just close your unlocked screen door, and nobody would bother your place.

Hoboes used to come around the house on Richards Street and rap on the door for a bite to eat, and we always gave them something. Dad always said, "Don't never turn anybody away hungry. Give them some bread or something."

My family never had a car, but some friends of my folks, the Crawfords, had a Model A Ford, and they'd come by and stay with us sometimes. Their son Holman was close buddies with Leon. He showed him how to drive a little bit, and then he drove Leon downtown. When they got there, he told him, "Okay, you drive back," and he left Leon with the car. The car had a clutch, and Leon wasn't too good with one of those yet, so the car was just lurching along. We were laughing about that. Holman's brother, Big Bill, became friends with me.

I got to come down to the United States a couple times when I was a kid. A good friend of my dad had a big car, and just for one day he drove the family across the border to Bellingham, Washington. Another time I came to Seattle with my mother, a reverend, two other women, and Frank, and we had dinner at a little restaurant over on 22nd and Madison. I was about twelve then, and Seattle seemed really big. I saw all the black kids on the street—at least it looked like a lot to me—and realized Seattle had more blacks than Vancouver. There were very few blacks in Vancouver in the '30s, and I knew all of them, even though they were

L<small>EON WITH HIS FRIENDS</small>
<small>IN</small> V<small>ANCOUVER.</small>

M<small>Y SISTER</small> P<small>AT AND HER DAUGHTER</small> G<small>RACIE</small>
<small>WALKING DOWN THE STREET.</small> T<small>HIS WAS TAKEN</small>
<small>BY A CAMERAMAN FOR THE</small> V<small>ANCOUVER</small> S<small>UN.</small>

scattered all over. Some of them lived on the East Side and a few lived right around the A.M.E. Church, but mostly a lot of white families lived in our neighborhood.

❧   ❧   ❧

 VERYBODY WAS shocked when my brother Leon suddenly died of a ruptured appendix when he was nineteen or twenty. That was in 1932, and it was so hard. Leon's was the first death in the family. When he was sick in bed, I'd come in from school and visit him up in his room before I'd go out to play.

Back then they gave people castor oil physics, although they found out later on that's the worst thing to do, especially with a stomachache. That's what my mother had been giving Leon at first, and then she was giving him enemas. The doctor came to see him and found out he had appendicitis and called for an ambulance. Leon died on the way to the hospital when his appendix ruptured.

I came home from school that day for lunch, and my mother told me that Leon had died. She told me that I didn't need to go back to school that afternoon. But a lot of people were coming to the house, so I said, "No, I think I'd rather go." I went back, but I was out of it.

It took a while for Leon's death to hit me, and then it was a miserable time. I started thinking to myself, "Gee, I won't see him anymore," and that's when it got to me. I went to the funeral, because that was something that had to be done. My brother Frank got very sick at the funeral.

It hit my mom hard, naturally, but it really tore my father up. Leon was my dad's favorite—that was his first child, and he'd done so many things. My dad had so many plans for Leon, including college, because he had already graduated from high school.

A couple of years after Leon's death, my father passed away from a heart problem, as I read from his death report. Maybe he died of a broken heart. He just pined so much over Leon. My mother used to tell him, "Well, you got two other sons."

He'd say, "Yeah, I know." But he had so much of his heart in Leon.

I got closer to my dad near the end. I'd hear him coughing upstairs in bed, and I'd run up to see if he needed anything. He'd ask me how I was doing and talk to me. He'd tell my brother and me, "You all be good boys and don't give your mother any trouble."

I said, "No, I won't."

My dad died at the hospital in 1934, when he was in his sixties or seventies. My mother, who died in 1984, lived a hundred years and eight months.

My brother Frank didn't go to my dad's funeral because he felt so bad. Mom and I tried to talk him into it, but he said that he didn't want to get sick again. We buried Leon and my father at the same place in Vancouver. I've forgotten through the years which cemetery it is, but they both have headstones. I've only been to the cemetery twice, and that was when they buried my brother and my dad. It was hard for me to get out there because I didn't have transportation and I didn't know where it was located.

After my dad died, we just went on with our lives, and I grew up real quick. It was rough. Dad was our only breadwinner, and mom took care of things at home while he was out working. My mother was easygoing but strong-willed, and after dad died she had to put up with a lot and just hung in there. Pat was helpful to my mom, because this sort of thing makes a family closer. Some people from the golf club gave my sister some part-time housework, and later on they gave Frank a job working Saturdays and Sundays at the golf course.

My mom started taking in laundry for a bachelor friend who went to our church and worked as a longshoreman. Then she took in other people's laundry. She also worked in Jean Fuller's after-hours chicken place on Friday and Saturday nights. Beer parlors and clubs would close up at midnight, so people would come by Jean Fuller's cafe, and she'd sell chicken dinners and drinks. My mother worked in the kitchen making salads and cooking. I started waiting tables at Jean Fuller's when I was in my teens. I'd do a little dancing in between and get tips from the patrons.

MY MOTHER AND PAT WITH MRS. WILSON.

We were still living at 1343 Richards Street when my dad passed away. My mother was paying a hundred dollars a month rent, and that was a lot of money. The landlord wouldn't cut down on the rent, even though he knew we were having such a hard time that we had to get on Canadian relief, which was like welfare. The old house started to deteriorate, but we stayed there for a while longer.

Around then the jitterbug craze came along, and Pat and I became more chummy. I began escorting her to parties and different events that Leon would have taken her to in the past. It got so I was moving into Pat's group of friends, and a lot of kids who didn't know us thought I was older than her. I'd take her to the midget car races too, because she liked those. She'd pay to get in, but I'd climb over the fence with the rest of the teenagers and meet her in the grandstands.

My brother Frank didn't go out a lot, although he'd go to a few parties. He was almost a wallflower. He could dance, but the gals would have to say, "C'mon, Frank." He wasn't forward like I was, and it was hard to get him into a conversation. As he grew older, though, he grew out of that. Frank was strange in some respects, even when we were kids. He'd blow up over certain things, and he wouldn't stand in a line, like at the store. I don't know what would overtake him to be like that, but that's the way he was.

Two years after my dad passed away we moved to 827 Georgia Street East. By then my mother was going with a guy named Mr. Moore, and we all moved into his house. Frank and I shared a double bed in a room with Big Bill Crawford, who was working on the railroad.

My mom did all the cooking for us. As times got tough, Mr. Moore would go down to the docks and get us salmon. When some of the boats came in, they'd put out big trays of salmon and give it away for free because the fish were just going to spoil. I ate so much salmon during the Dirty Thirties!

The house had a back yard that Mr. Moore was always digging up and planting. Most of the people around the neighborhood had their veggies growing out in back. We had beans, corn, lettuce, tomatoes, cabbage, rhubarb. The whole family worked on it, and I hated it. I didn't like to do the weeding or the watering.

That's why I was surprised when I took up landscape gardening while Jimmy was growing up. Of course, landscape gardening was a little different—mostly I did a lot of lawn mowing and hedge trimming—but I did find that I like to work outdoors.

Whenever I could, I'd make a little extra money hauling wood and sawdust for some East Indian Hindus who had a wood yard. I drove a flatbed truck for them, and two or three of us would haul sawdust in big hundred-pound sacks. I also worked in their sawmill, sorting out the edging from the finer types of wood. The work paid a dollar a day, and over-time didn't mean anything. Nowadays you hear guys say, "Ooh, that job don't pay enough—I don't want it." Man, back when I was coming along, if we'd see a sign for a job—wow! You'd have to fight for it, and you wouldn't be asking how much it paid.

❧   ❧   ❧

I ALWAYS LISTENED to the old *Midnight Prowl*, a radio show that came on around twelve o'clock. It featured a lot of the big bands—Duke Ellington, Benny Goodman, Artie Shaw. The only big band I ever saw in Canada was Duke Ellington's, and in 1936 my sister and I got our pictures right on the front page of the *Vancouver Sun* dancing to his music. That was during the jitterbug craze, and he played at the Arena. He was up there doing his thing, and I was out on the floor doing my thing when they snapped the photo. My regular jitterbug partner was so mad about not getting her picture on the front page.

I thought about going to get an autograph from Duke, but in between the sessions people were all crowding around, reaching up there with their pieces of paper and pens, and he looked so tired. The sweat was coming off his brow and he had a frozen smile on his face. I said, "Gee, that guy's going through a lot of hassle." I felt sorry for him.

I had a zoot suit, with the peg-legged pants, jive chain, and Big Apple hat. I didn't get mine too extreme, though—I had kind of conservative drapes. My fanciest suit was brown with white pinstripes. I'd wear that dancing. I also had a beige coat, single-breasted with only one button. It was not too extremely long, but a little longer than the coats of today. I was cool!

I loved dancing, and I was quite a jitterbugger. I'd still like to do it. I have that feeling of what I want to do, but the old joints won't correspond with what's running in my brain. I used to really do some jumping. I'd flip the gal in the air and slide her between my legs or bounce her off my knee. It's a strenuous, acrobatic dance. I had two dance partners. I first started dancing with Beverly Estes, a good tap dancer who'd danced in the States. My other partner was Dorothy King, and we went to functions and danced together as a team. We liked doing a lot of swinging. For a while I even had an agent and tap danced solo at some Vancouver clubs. A white band would hire me to be the entertainment while they were resting during the intermission. That was easy money, because I'd get paid five dollars a night for that—shoot, that was big money! Most of the functions I danced at were all-white; I'd be about the only black in the bunch. All those people talked to me, though, and I'd yackety-yack with them.

I also did a lot of dancing when some of the black people would put on shows to raise money. In one particular show that Jean Fuller put on, Beverly Estes and I were playing people who were supposed to be getting married. It was set up as a musical, with regular rhymes. Somebody on the sideline would say, "Here they come!" and we'd come trucking up the aisle and then do our thing as the bridesmaids did their thing. Any little function that came along, I'd get in there and perform.

Another time I was in a jitterbug contest with Dorothy King at the Orpheum Theater. One week they had some jitterbugs from the States, showing the different moves, and then they announced a jitterbug contest. My friend Buster Keeling, his girlfriend Edna, Dorothy, and I signed up. The contest was wide open to everybody, but when we went down there, they didn't contest us against the whites because the whites, they said, didn't have a chance against us. I said, "Oh, man, ain't this something." So we didn't do any dancing at all, but they paid us twenty-five dollars and we split the money.

The dances all originated down in the States, and then they'd come up to Vancouver and we'd grab ahold of them. I was dancing every new step that came through via vaudeville artists like Ham & Eggs and the Nicholas Brothers, who were top-quality tap dancers. I'd also pick up on all of Bill Robinson's stuff in the motion pictures, like the routine where he danced up and down the steps. I'd go to see all the movies he made by himself or with Shirley Temple. I'd see any dancing picture two or three times. I'd just sit there, watching one show after the other.

I got to be a visitor at school, as my mother used to say. I was around seventeen when I just lost interest. I got to feeling that it didn't make any difference what position I got in—I still couldn't get a good-paying job. It just seemed hopeless. I knew I needed the education, but as far as going to a university goes, there just was no way. There just wasn't money to be doing all that.

I tried boxing to make some money, and unintentionally wound up fighting in the 1936 Golden Gloves. A welterweight named Al Ford called me on the phone one day and said, "Would you like to make some money, Al?"

"Yeah! Heck, yeah. I'm broke all the time."

"You got to do some fighting for it."

"Well, I can go along with that."

"You get paid twenty-five dollars a round."

I said, "What? Yeah!"

"Three rounds."

"Shoot! That's seventy-five dollars."

He gave me an address and said everything would be taken care of. I was all excited. When I got there, I ran into a friend of mine, Muggy Jones. I said, "Hey, Muggy. What's going on? What you doing over here too?"

"There's a fight fest going on." He didn't tell me it was the Golden Gloves, though. And the Golden Gloves, I knew, were amateur matches and the fighters don't get paid anything.

I met some of the other guys, and we piled into two cars they had to take us down to the States. Still nobody said anything about the Golden Gloves. They said something about us going to Portland, Oregon. We rode down to the border—I was sitting on a welterweight's lap all the way, and that was a long haul—and then they told us the fights had been can-celed in Portland and we were going to Seattle. The hotel in downtown Seattle was all taken care of by the managers handling us.

Besides Muggy and me, the rest of the group was white. This hotel had a swimming pool, so a few of us decided to take a dip. When we went to get our towels, Muggy and I were told, "You black guys can't go in the pool, but the white guys are allowed." The guys we were with said, "If they can't go, we're not going either," and they didn't go. They thought it was crazy, although they did

Maso Ono, Harry Hastings, and me in 1935. Maso was Japanese, Harry was Scotch Canadian, and I'm the one with the tie. I'd just come from Sunday school when my sister took this picture.

have similar prejudices in Vancouver. Blacks, Chinese, Japanese, East Indians, and members of any other ethnic race weren't allowed to swim at the Crystal Pool on Beach Avenue. It was a public pool, but only Caucasians could swim there.

The fights were held on Second Avenue overlooking the Puget Sound. When they announced that we were there for the Golden Gloves, I said, "Oh, no! Damn! We don't get paid anything." I fought as a lightweight and reached the finals, but I just didn't have my heart in it.

After that I got involved in a homesteading deal that turned out to be a fiasco. I was eighteen, and I still wasn't working or doing anything in Vancouver. By then Buster Keeling was married and running on the railroad. His mother-in-law started telling me about how they came from out in the country in Alberta. She also did a lot of talking about horses, so Buster wanted to get some land where he could raise horses. He told me, "Al, you should come along and help me build a log cabin," so I went up there with him and an older guy, Mr. Cephas, who knew the way.

We crossed to the north shore of Vancouver and caught a freight train up to Lone Butte, riding on top of the cars all through the mountains. Lone Butte was way up near the end of the line. From there we had to walk through the woods. We had a .22 rifle, and after our other food ran out we shot rabbits, squirrels, and birds for survival. We had our packs on our back, and I had a nice warm overcoat. At night we just rolled up in our blankets on the ground. Mr. Cephas couldn't read or write, but he knew his way around in the woods.

Finally we came to a place owned by a white family named Miller. They were from the States. Mr. Miller was from the South, and when he first saw Buster, he said, "Man, I haven't seen any of you"—meaning blacks—"for a long time!"

Then he saw all three of us and said, "Well, what y'all doing up here?"

Mr. Miller and his wife had two young boys. Buster and Mr. Cephas stayed there a couple of days, and then they went on to see Buster's land. As they were leaving, Buster told me that he'd be sending me some money to get back home. They ended up going back to Vancouver without me, and I stayed with the Millers for two or three months, working for my keep. It was just like back in the settler days, living in a log cabin with no electricity and a floor hewn from logs. I learned how to milk a cow and slop hogs. They had a couple of horses, and I rode bareback a lot. Buster never sent any money, so finally I told Mrs. Miller that I had to go back. I sold her a couple of blankets to get the money for the ferry from North Vancouver. The mailman brought me down to Lone Butte in his Tin Lizzie, and then I just watched for the train and jumped aboard.

❧   ❧   ❧

THERE WASN'T nothing happening for me in Canada. I tried to get a job on the railroad, because my brother got one. It seemed like everybody got on the railroad but me. For two years in a row I went down there and applied. I passed the Red Cross medical examination they gave the guys in case of an emergency. They'd teach you how to break down a berth on the train, and I passed that. I always passed everything, but the head of the porters just had it in for me. He'd tell me I was too short. Every year he'd say, "Well, maybe next year you'll grow some more."

I said, "Hell, I ain't gonna grow no more." I wasn't getting any taller after I got around eighteen. I was the shortest man in the family. I was taller than my mother and sister, but shorter than my dad and brothers. Jimmy was taller than me too—he was around 5'9". On top of that, I was taller than some of the porters that they already had. Some of those guys had to stand on the rests in the coaches to unlock the upper berths, but I could do it standing flat-foot. That guy sure was a jinx to me.

I couldn't get other jobs because of prejudice. One crazy rule the Canadian government had was that nobody could have a government job—like working with the Post Office or anything like that—unless they or their parents came from the old country, like England or Scotland. Even if you were a Canadian-born black or Indian, you couldn't get a government job.

I just wanted to get out of Vancouver and see more people. I wanted to see more blacks, for one thing! I saw a few of the guys around town marrying the gals. There weren't that many blacks in Vancouver, and we all knew each other practically from childhood. There wasn't much of a selection unless a new girl moved to town. I knew a lot of gals, but I didn't have a steady girlfriend. Some of them used to yackety-yack with me, but I was too slow for them. I didn't want to get tied down and all serious with anyone, because I had plans to see the world. I'd read the black newspapers that came to town with the railroad porters, like the *Pittsburgh Courier* and *Chicago Defender*. They'd have a lot about black entertainers and black gals, and I'd say, "Wow! I'd sure like to get to the

United States, where I could see more blacks."

Sometimes I'd ask my mother, "What was it like going to an all-black school?" because I'd remember that's what she went to in the South. During the time she was coming along in Georgia and Tennessee, it was all segregated. Mom said, "I did all right, but you've got a lot more opportunities here because there's no segregation at Canadian schools."

I was the youngest one in my family, and I was the first one to leave home. I told my mom, "Shoot, I gotta get out of here." This was right when the World War II was coming on. I said, "If I don't get away from here now, they'll get me in the army, and then they won't let me go anywhere."

I went to Victoria first. A friend of mine, Dee Meyers, had gone there from Vancouver, and he seemed to be doing pretty good. He told me, "Yeah, we could shack up together in the same place. I been trying to hold down two jobs. You could take over one of them and make some money." The job was shining shoes, so that's what I did. I didn't tell Dee what my idea was, though. I was just trying to make enough money to get out of town. We shared a room, and I was only there for two or three months.

I came to live in Seattle in 1940. Having dual citizenship made it easy for me. I was born in Vancouver, but my father didn't take out naturalization papers in Canada until after I was born. I was the youngest one, so all of us siblings had the opportunity to either be American or Canadian. I had gone to the American Immigration in Vancouver and asked them what it would take for me to become a citizen. The guy said, "You have to have fifteen hundred dollars"—which was out of the question for me—"or you need to have a sponsor who can take care of you financially or provide living quarters." I knew a few people in Seattle, and some of them knew me all my life, but they weren't financially able to do that for me, and I

wasn't going to ask them. "Oh, well," I thought, "I'll just have to make a little stake and go down there on my own."

And that's what I did. I had around forty dollars when I came to Seattle. When that ran out, I didn't let anybody know. One family, the Clarks, had known me ever since I was a kid out there in the house where I was born. So I had my mail from my mother sent there. When I'd go to pick it up, I'd sit there and talk with Mrs. Clark. Her son Jimmy was working on the ships, and I'd see him once in a while. He got me signed up to go out on the ships, so I'd sit around the Seaman's Hall, trying to ship out as part of the Marine Cooks and Stewards, but I never did get on any ships until after the war.

Some other people in Seattle, the Hardings, also knew me when I was a kid. As a matter of fact, Mrs. Harding was a first cousin to Louis Armstrong, and she had a picture of Louis sitting on a side table. I went over to her place and told her that I was in Seattle to stay and needed some work. So the Hardings had me work around their house. I'd clean, vacuum, wash windows, mow the lawn, and weed. I made extra money doing housecleaning and yard work for Mrs. Harding's neighbor. I'd work as a handyman for their friends and mow lawns around the neighborhood. I was doing every-thing I could to make some money. My mother didn't have any money to send me, and I wasn't going to be sponging off of anybody. I wanted to work my way because that's what my dad always taught me.

I found odd jobs through the paper, clean-ing houses and washing windows for thirty-five cents an hour. Then I started working regularly at Ben Paris, a restaurant on Pike Street. I worked the night shift, shining shoes, bussing tables, and cleaning the place. From there, I got a job as a laborer on the day shift at an iron foundry. ❧

I WAS WORKING AT the foundry when I met Jimmy's mother, Lucille Jeter, in 1941. At the time I was living with some friends of mine who'd come from Canada too— Donald Green and his sister Christina. The landlady's oldest girl, Berthelle, knew Lucille because they went to the same high school, and she brought her home one Friday night when I was getting ready to go to a dance. One of the big bands was playing at the Washington Club.

Berthelle brought her in and said, "Al, I want you to meet Lucille."

THAT'S LUCILLE AND JIMMY. LUCILLE WROTE ON THE BACK, "DEAR MOTHER, I AM SENDING YOU A PICTURE OF THE BABY AND I. WE WILL BE UP THERE IN THE NEXT COUPLE WEEKS, SO LOOK FOR US. LOVE." I THINK THIS WAS SENT TO MY MOTHER, ALTHOUGH LUCILLE AND JIMMY DIDN'T MEET HER UNTIL AFTER THE WAR.

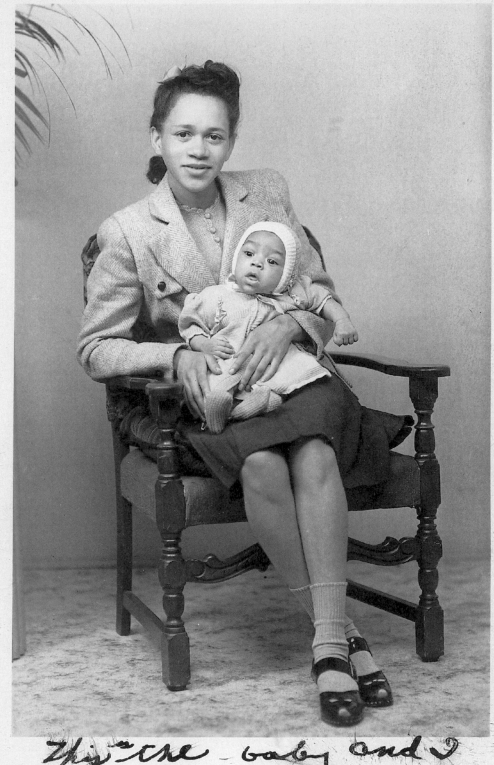

This "the baby and I

Lucille
Hendrix

33

"Hi."

I wasn't even thinking of taking anybody to the dance, but we got to yackety-yacking, and Berthelle said, "Why don't you take Lucille to the dance?"

I thought she was kind of young for Berthelle to be saying that! Lucille was close to seventeen, and I was about six years older. I said, "Well...," and I asked Lucille, "Can you go to the dance? It's a grown-up place. Do your parents know you'll be out? You'll probably have to go home and change clothes."

"Oh, yeah," Lucille said, "everything'll be fine with my family." So I took her to the dance.

I started jumping around there on the dance floor and forgot about Lucille. Berthelle said to me, "Al, you're ignoring Lucille. She's over there, and nobody will dance with her." I guess she looked too young to be there, and people wouldn't dance with her.

"Oh, dadgum," I said. I went over and apologized, and we spent the rest of the evening together.

This guy was going around with a camera, and Donald and his girlfriend, Berthelle, and Lucille and I sat down on a couch and had our picture taken together. I paid for the picture and said, "I'm going to get some copies made." Donald got ahold of it and lost track of it, so I never did get the picture back. It made me so mad for a good while. I said, "Gee, I wish I could get that back!" That was way back there, the first time we went out, and I wanted to see what we looked like.

There wasn't nothing there at first with Lucille—she was so young! But some girls like older guys, I guess, and Lucille and I started seeing each other a good deal. I started kissing her after the second or third time I saw her, and I started having some romantic feelings for her. She'd come by nearly every day after I'd come home from work. Then I had a hernia at the iron foundry, and they had to take me to the hospital emergency room. It was on a Friday, and I was getting ready to go out that night too.

While I was in Harborview Hospital, Lucille came to see me every day. Lucille would bring me some kind of something, and I thought that was nice. It made me feel real good.

Lucille was a good-looking girl with a nice smile. She was very pretty and had fair skin. She was on the slim side, but she wasn't all that frail. She wasn't sickly, like some people have written. She had a good constitution, although over time she ran it down. She was a good dresser when she had money to dress up.

Lucille had a good sense of humor—she was jovial—and we liked to joke around. She'd say things to me like, "Yeah, you Canadians. You tell 'em a joke today and next week they get the joke and start laughing."

I'd say, "No, you're the one that's like that." Because I'd tell her something sometimes, she'd laugh, and then I'd say, "You didn't get it, did you?"

Everybody's got a certain amount of stubbornness to them when they get their mind set to something, and Lucille was no different. But even when we were disagreeing, she'd see my point in a lot of ways. She didn't rebel against her parents. I'd tell her, "Now you mind your parents. Regardless of how you feel about a lot of things, they're usually right." That's the way I was brought up, and Jimmy was too.

Lucille's folks would want me to visit them, so I'd go by and eat and sit and talk with them. They were very fond of me. Lucille's dad, Preston Jeter, was a gruff little old guy who reminded me of Wallace Beery, the actor. He was hefty and grumpy and defensive, which is a natural way with fathers anyway. Mr. Jeter talked about being a longshoreman, but when I knew him he was retired and didn't do anything. He was kind of a bluffer, but we had good conversations. He was trying to look rough and tough, but he was easy underneath.

He died during the war.

Lucille's mother, Clarice Jeter, was always wanting me to hang around too, so I'd be at their place a long time. Mrs. Jeter had been the housekeeper for a family I knew in Seattle, the Hurds. When I knew her, though, she didn't do any work either, and the family just lived on welfare. Mrs. Jeter was easygoing and laid-back. She didn't argue about anything. She believed in taking life easy. I think her maiden name was Lawson. Like Lucille, she was slender and fair-skinned. Jimmy liked her, and he always called her Grandma. When he was little she'd take him to the show and to church, and he knew her until she passed away when he was a teenager.

Mrs. Jeter was religious, and she belonged to the Father Diviners. Father Divine was a black guy who came out of obscurity—nobody seemed to know where he came from. He was an American, and he had followers in Canada and down through the States. He was a big, well-known person, and a lot of people called him God and all such as that. He didn't only have a black following; he had all races following him. When I was a kid, some friends of ours were also followers of Father Divine. When you'd go up to their place, the first thing they'd say to you as they opened the door was "Peace, brother." Father Divine had a lot of eating places where you could get meals a whole lot cheaper than elsewhere—fifteen cents, or if you didn't have any money they'd still feed you. There was one of those places in Seattle on Madison Street. Clarice Jeter would always say, "Oh, Father Divine!" She didn't drink any alcohol, and I never saw Lucille's dad drink either.

Lucille had brothers and sisters—Dolores, Clifford, Gertrude, and Nancy, who we sometimes called Anne. Nancy was the closest to Lucille's age, and she was the only one who was still living at home when Lucille and I were going out. I didn't know Gertrude at all. I only saw Gertrude and her husband about three times. She was much older than Dolores, who was only a month older than me.

It went on to where Lucille and I just became attached. Whenever someone mentioned one of us, they'd mention both of us—Al and Lucille, Lucille and Al. When any functions came up, we would always go together. Naturally we jitterbugged together at some of the parties and dances, but Lucille and I didn't do any special-type dancing like I'd done in Vancouver with my partners.

Mostly I was busy keeping my nose to the grindstone, trying to keep a job going. After I got out of the hospital, I wasn't able to go back to that job at the foundry because it was a lot of heavy work, and I'd just had that hernia operation. Right downstairs from where I lived at 2028 Madison was a place called Honeysuckle's Pool Hall. I enjoyed playing eight-ball, straight pool, and nine-ball, and I knew the owner of the place, so he gave me a job racking balls. There wasn't a whole lot of work to it, no lifting, so I did pretty good at that. That's what I was doing when Uncle Sam came along and got me.

I was racking balls at Honeysuckle's on the Sunday when Pearl Harbor was attacked. Of course, when the news came over the radio, it seemed like nobody around there knew where Pearl Harbor was. Somebody said, "Where in the heck is Pearl Harbor?"

Not long after that they started talking about rounding up Japanese people in the United States to send them to relocation centers. I thought it was terrible. I said, "Damn! If Japanese people were born and raised here, hell, they should leave them alone." I knew a lot of Japanese in Canada. I ran around with a lot of Japanese kids—Maso and his whole family—and I knew that it was nothing but racism. It had to be. They didn't do it to the Germans or the Italians. A few years earlier, there was an import and export store on Hastings Street in Vancouver, and there were espionage and anti-

American activities going on in there. As we'd go walking by, some of them people would come out of the store and give the old Hitler salute—heil! I said, "Damn! Now here they're picking on the innocent Japanese, while these other people were just flaunting it. Ain't that something?"

I especially didn't care for the way Hitler was taking over and the Nazis were killing off people. Hitler kept talking about the "master race," and yet he had the Italians and the Japanese on his side. I kept thinking, "If they were to win and take over everything, Hitler would be sure to get the cream of the crop. Maybe for a while after that the Germans and Italians and Japanese would live in harmony, but then they'd be at each other's throats." Those thoughts were always in my mind—and there ain't no such thing as a master race!

Canada did the same thing to the Japanese. Maso Ono and his three brothers and two sisters were born in Canada, but their parents were born in Japan, so the whole Ono family was rounded up and put in internment camps. During the war I lost contact with Maso, and then I heard that they had him in the service as an interpreter for the Canadian forces since he could read and speak Japanese.

I was classified I-A even before I had a physical. When I got my draft notice and classification from the U.S. government, they

told me that there wasn't anything for me to do, no papers to sign. I wasn't tempted to go back to Vancouver, because that's what I wanted to get away from. I didn't want to get into the Canadian army because if I did, I'd have been really stuck up there. My brother Frank went into the Canadian army and was sent to an anti-aircraft battery on an island off the coast near Vancouver. Mom stayed with Mr. Moore in Vancouver, and he died during the war. Mom stayed in his house and eventually started going with a guy named Reddick.

I moved to a rooming house on 23rd Avenue. I wasn't allowed to have any women there, unless they were sitting in the parlor —the landlady didn't go for any hanky-panky. So when Lucille and I wanted time alone, we'd take walks. She didn't live very far from Garfield High School, and we would walk that way or over to where I lived.

Right around the time that I got my induction notice, Lucille found out she was pregnant with Jimmy. As I was going over to her place, she came running down the street and told me, "Oh, I missed my period."

"Oops."

I knew then that she was pregnant. I wasn't looking for it to happen, but I wasn't scared, because I had planned on marrying her.

Then Lucille said, "Oh, dad's so mad, I don't know if you should go over to the house," because she had already told him.

I said, "Well, I expected something like that.

I'm not going to be shunning him. I've got to face up to him sometime, so I'm going to go over there now."

Mr. Jeter was rather perturbed. Lucille was the youngest daughter, and here she was having the first child. He was fuming around, but he didn't bellow "You got my daughter pregnant!" or do any of that. I told him how I felt: "I'll take care of your daughter. I was planning on marrying Lucille anyhow. I'm going to stand up and do her right. I'll be going in the army soon, so I can make an allotment to her and the baby."

Lucille's mother and I were closer, and it didn't bother her that Lucille was pregnant. She was happy about it, because before that she was always saying in a joking way, "Ooh, when you all gonna get married?"

I'd just say, "Oh, one of these days." Lucille was happy about being pregnant too.

I wanted to get all married up before I went in the service, so our ceremony was a quickie. All we had to do was get five dollars for a marriage license and then go to a justice of the peace at the Seattle courthouse. No one from our families was there, and we didn't even take a witness with us. It was just Lucille and me, and one of the clerks stood in as a witness. It was the first time I ever got married, and I was in a daze, like most guys. I thought to myself, "Now I got a wife. I'm taking on responsibility for someone else."

Lucille and I didn't have time to make any plans for the baby, because Uncle Sam had my plans all made. We got married on March 31, and I went in the service three days later on April 3, 1942. I tried to get deferred, but it didn't work. If Lucille had been further along in her pregnancy, I might have gotten a little more time at home.

There was a club in Seattle called the Rocking Chair, just a hole-in-the-wall where mostly blacks would go, although it was open to anybody. I didn't frequent the place too much,

but just before I went in the service Lucille and I went there. Of course, they didn't know she was underage. I told the guy at the door, "Oh, yeah. That's my wife." It was a little splurge, because the next day I had to go. Lucille and I never lived together until after the war.

❧　❧　❧

THE NEXT morning I caught the bus downtown and checked in at the Armory. We took buses to Fort Lewis, just on the other side of Tacoma, where we were inducted. There were eight of us from Seattle. We went to Fort Sill, Oklahoma, and that's where I got my basic training with the field artillery. I was on a 155-millimeter howitzer, and I learned to shoot a .50-caliber machine gun, but I didn't get any action where I had to use them. Those guns were sure loud when you're sitting on top of them, but they didn't think about earplugs. Even when you were firing the howitzers, they'd just tell you to put your hands over your ears and open up your mouth and scream.

They didn't have mixed troops like they do now. There were all-black units and all-white units. Of course, all of our commissioned officers for the black units were white—that's from lieutenant second grade on up. The non-coms like corporal, master sergeant, and first sergeant were black.

After basic training, they split us up. From Oklahoma I went to Fort Benning, Georgia. That was an experience. We ran into Jim Crow on the train. Before we got to the Mason-Dixon line, eight of us had a whole car to ourselves. We walked where we wanted, and we were sitting and looking out the windows on either side of the train. After we made a switchover somewhere close to the line, I noticed little slots on the back of some of the seats in one small section. I was wondering what those things were for.

I soon found out. After we crossed the line, a different conductor came aboard. We were sitting all over the car, and this guy said, "Okay, you guys. All you boys gotta get back over there." The slots meant Negroes on one side, while whites sat on the other. So we were all crammed into this small area, and that's the way it was until we got to Fort Benning.

When we got to the camp, they just put us to one side because so many troops were coming in they didn't have room to send us to the regular units. I was at Fort Benning for a month or longer, and I still wasn't assigned to a particular unit. We were in barracks and got our meals and gear, but we didn't get paid. We didn't even have soap or anything like that. A spokesman for our outfit finally talked to some of the command- ing officers, and one of the officers said, "We'll see what we can do to get you some toiletries and money for ciga- rettes." So they did give us some canteen books one time. You'd sign for a five- or ten-dollar canteen book with tick- ets in it, and you could buy things from the PX with them.

At Fort Benning the blacks had to stay on one side, and the whites stayed on the other. Any bus that came onto the fort to carry soldiers to town on the weekend had segregated sections too. Blacks had to wait until all the white soldiers got on, and if there was any room for them in the black section, then they could get on. If there wasn't, you'd have to wait

PFC James Allen Hendrix.

until the next bus. That's the way it went.

Being at Fort Benning was almost like a vacation, because they didn't have anything for us to do. I didn't do any training, so in my idle time I'd go down around the river to see the paratroopers jumping out of planes or training with stationary parachutes. Mostly, though, we were just sitting around. What they were doing was putting a bunch of guys to one side for this new facility they were getting together in Alabama—Camp Rucker.

When I got there, Camp Rucker was spanking brand-new. It had been built on a peanut plantation. They had bulldozed the fields, but you could see where the peanuts had been. They told me to go to a certain barracks, and that's where I ran into Sergeant Taylor, a staff sergeant and an old soldier who'd been in the service a long time. He was a cavalry man too, so we struck it off real good and eventually went overseas together. I found out from him that they were in the process of making up a new unit called the Airbase Security Battalion. We were supposed to take care of airstrips for fighters and bombers.

As one of the first arrivals, I had this great big barracks all to myself. I could get any bunk and pick whichever spot I wanted. A few days later a whole bunch of troops started coming in, and they started forming up and giving out promotions. Sergeant Taylor wanted to make a corporal out of me. I said, "No. I'm gonna just stay a private. I don't want no responsibility."

He said, "What about PFC?"

"Do you have to make those non-com meetings?"

"No."

So I said, "Okay, you can make me a PFC." I was a PFC—private first class—the whole war.

I found out that our new unit was going to be assigned half-tracks with heavy 75-millimeter guns, like the old famous French 75s of the first World War. They had one of those on each half-track, and some had .50-caliber machine guns. We were going to be attached to the Eighth Air Force, and wherever they went, we went. We would guard the airstrips, the planes, and the bomb dumps.

I'd pray every day that everything would be okay with Lucille and our baby. She wanted to come down to where I was, but I wrote and told her, "No, I don't want you in Alabama."

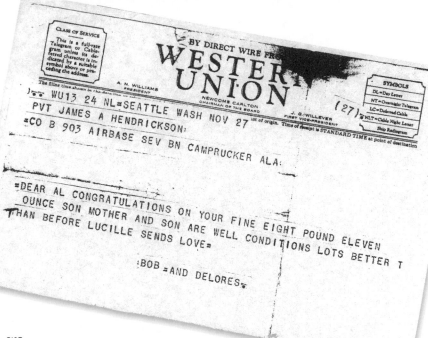

❧   ❧   ❧

NE OF THE happiest moments of my life was when Jimmy was born. I found out when I got a telegram from Lucille's sister Dolores. At the time, I was in the stockade.

When they read to you the Articles of War, they tell you that you can go home for a sickness, birth, and death. When it was coming around time for Jimmy to be born, I went to the commanding officer and expressed that my wife was going to have a baby and I'd like to get a furlough. At the time they were giving some of the guys furloughs, but I was just too far away from home. Everything was by railroads—there wasn't any flying—and they were only giving five days' leave. That was okay for the guys who lived right around Alabama, but I was the only one in my outfit from Seattle. So my commanding officer said, "Hendrix, you just don't have enough time to get home in five days. You'd just get there and have to turn right around and come back. Sorry, but you can't go home."

I fired him a salute and started out the door. He stopped me and said, "Hendrix!"

"Yes, sir."

"And don't go over the hill." In other words, don't go AWOL.

I was so doggone far away from home, shoot, there wasn't much chance of me getting there. And I'm down there in Alabama? That's rough. I told him, "No, sir," and I left.

The next day they told me I was going to the stockade. I asked the sergeant what I was going to the stockade for, and he said, "I don't know. I'm just asking this MP to take you there."

It's not on my record, but I was in the stockade about a month and a half. I didn't have a trial of any sort. I just stayed in the compound and did close-order drill all through the day.

Then one day at mail call, I got a Western Union telegram. I said, "Now who in the heck sent me a telegram?" When you got a telegram in those days, it usually meant bad news, so I said, "Ooh-wee."

I sat down on the bunk to read it. It was from my sister-in-law Dolores and her husband Bob up in Seattle. It was addressed to "Private James A. Hendrickson" and dated November 27, 1942. The telegram said, "Dear

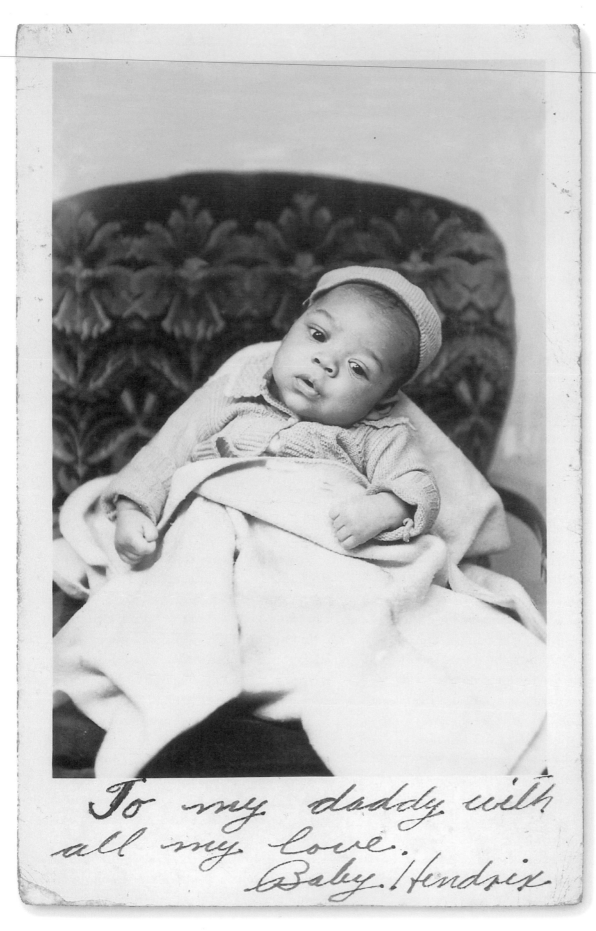

To my daddy with all my love. Baby Hendrix

I GOT THIS POSTCARD PHOTO WHEN I WAS IN THE SERVICE, AND I CARRIED IT IN MY TRUNK ALL THROUGH THE WAR. (THE BACK IS SHOWN AT RIGHT.)

Al. Congratulations on your fine eight pound eleven ounce son. Mother and son are well. Conditions lots better than before. Lucille sends love. Bob and Dolores."

I shouted, "Wow! Hey, guys—lookee here! I've become a dad!"

They were saying congratulations and slapping me on the back. It was a pleasant surprise, and after that I was always thinking about what my son looked like. I thought, "Oh, man, it's going to be strange—I hope he don't get too old before I get home."

When my outfit got ready to go overseas, they let me go back to the barracks to get my gear together, and then I spent one more night in the stockade. The next day I joined up with my outfit, and we headed out for San Francisco to get ready to go overseas.

Once I shipped out, I didn't lose pay for the time that I was in the stockade, because they didn't have anything on me. I figure they were just holding me there to keep me from going over the hill. I asked my first sergeant, "What the heck was I in the stockade for?"

"General principle," he said, "general principle."

At that time we were getting, as they say, "twenty-one dollars a day, once a month." So when I finally got paid, I had three months coming. I was well-heeled then, but I sent most of it home. I just kept enough for cigarettes. One good thing was cigarettes were cheap. You'd get a carton of cigarettes—mine were Lucky Strikes—for fifty cents from the PX. I smoked a pack a day all through the war.

They shipped us out from Frisco on January 7, 1943. During the voyage across the Pacific, I'd walk around, look at the horizon, and yackety-yack. We'd play cards, shoot dice. Guys were always asking, "Have you got any money?" They had lots of card games and crap games going.

The first places we stopped were New Caledonia and New Hebrides, but we didn't disembark. We arrived in the Fiji Islands on January 21st. I liked the Fijis. It was nice because we could leave the ship and associate around with people. They let us go ashore in Suva, the capital, and gave each soldier a five-dollar bill and said, "Compliments of President Roosevelt." They also told us, "Okay,

you guys stick together and be back at the ship at such-and-such a time." I just took it easy. I wanted to look at the sights, which were interesting. Some of the guys came back loaded, but we didn't have any AWOLs.

I ended up spending part of my service soldiering in the Fijis, where there wasn't really a threat from the enemy. Our outfit was called the 903rd Airbase Security Battalion, and I was

Taken Feb. 20, 1943

Dear Allan;
Here at last, is a picture of your little boy Allan Hendrix. He is exactly 2 months and three weeks old. He looks twice as s____ ____ ____ he? I hope you will receive it O.K.
Velora Hall

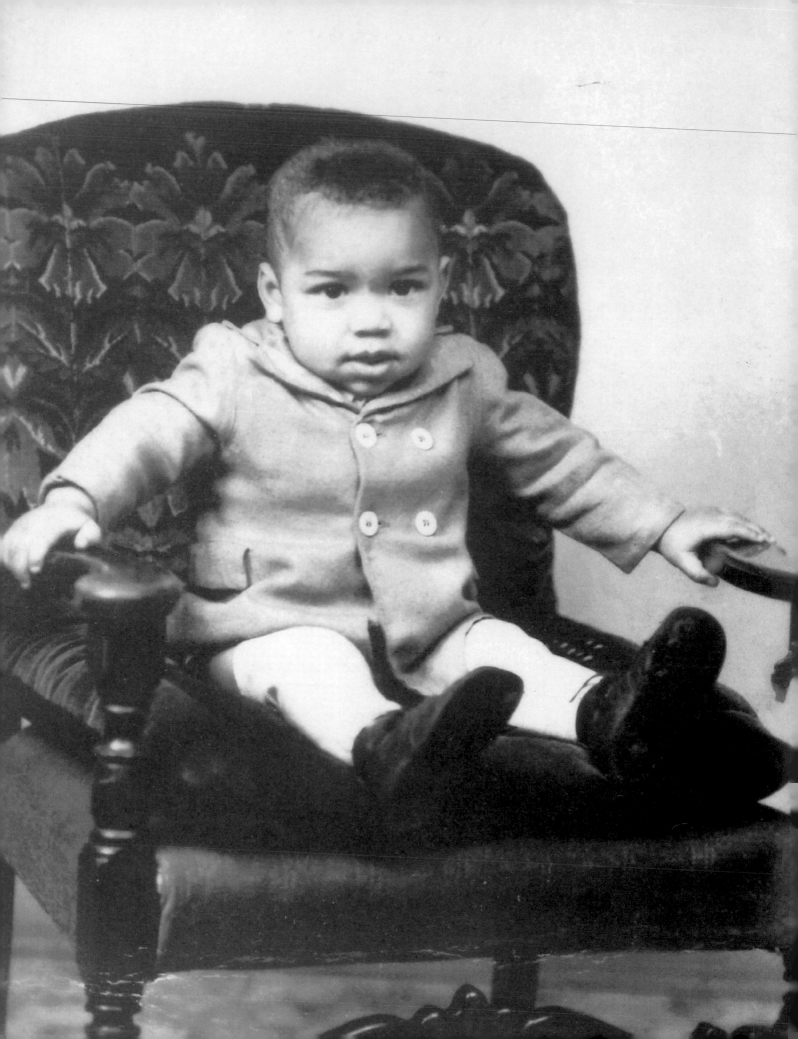

in Company B. We just did guard duty at bomb dumps and airstrips and other military facilities. I saw my first Flying Fortress there. That was the largest plane around, and it looked *big*. I also saw Jack Benny and Carole Landis performing with the USO while I was stationed in the Fiji Islands.

I shared a tent with Sergeant Taylor and two other guys. Sergeant Taylor was my closest friend in the service. He was down-to-earth, and he had a family. During time off, we'd goof around in the area—there was always something to do. At least we could go to the villages and see some women dance around! As the war progressed, we didn't see any women for a long time, because we started going to islands like Guadalcanal, where they always moved all the women away from the villages, so only the men were around.

I got a bad case of tonsillitis in the Fijis. I was hardly able to swallow water. The doctor said, "When the swelling goes down, I'm going to have those tonsils taken out, because they're real bad." But when the swelling went down, he never took them out. I just told myself, "I'm going to have to try to keep from getting a cold," because my throat was the first place a cold would go. One of the first things I did when I got out of the service was go to the Marine Hospital and have my tonsils taken out.

The first time I saw a photo of Jimmy was overseas. Dolores sent me a little picture of my son and his cousin Roberta on a blanket. Roberta was Dolores' first daughter. Another picture was of Lucille and Jimmy. Lucille still looked real young. I also had a photo of Jimmy in his grandmother Jeter's arms. All the time I was in the service, I had Jimmy's pictures in my footlocker and billfold. Naturally I prayed for Jimmy every day I was in the service.

I finally left the Fijis on October 10, 1943.

Jimmy in his Aunt Dolores' chair, 1944.

We were on the water for seven days before we put a foot on dry land. During those seven days we stopped by New Hebrides, but we didn't get off. On October 17th, we arrived in Guadalcanal. It was all secured by then, but there were still a lot of battle scars around, like bombed-out amphibious vehicles. We were stationed by the Henderson airstrip, which had a P.O.W. camp nearby. I saw the Japanese P.O.W.s, but we weren't allowed to talk to them or make any contact.

We didn't stay in Guadalcanal too long, and I served the rest of my time in the service guarding airstrips in New Guinea. They didn't have any cities out where we were by Melanie Bay. Tropical—that's all it was! We were doing a little bit of everything. The war was winding down, so we unloaded and loaded ships. We destroyed a lot of government property, burning some of the shacks that the troops had used. The natives could have used them afterwards, but the government wouldn't allow that. We got bombed a few times at the airbase at Melanie Bay, but the Japanese planes would mostly come over to harass us. They liked to break up our shows. We'd be out there at night with the Seabees and the Marines watching outdoor theater, and a plane would come over and all the lights would have to go out. We'd jump into the bomb shelters, and the Japanese would bomb us for a while. We'd stay in the shelters until the siren sounded all clear, and then we'd go back to watch the show. But the Japanese never did make any frontal attack where we had to get down to the nitty-gritty and do a whole lot of shooting. I'm glad of that part.

I didn't hate the Japanese in any way, shape, or form, but I believed in what we were fighting for. I just hated being in the service on account of it taking me away from my home life. Having a son made me more anxious to get home. I felt a responsibility to be there for Jimmy, and there was never a moment of doubt that I wanted to get home to be there for him.

IF OR A WHILE Lucille was writing all the time. After Jimmy was born, she had a hard time. I knew it was going to be hard on her by herself, and I know she tried to get help from the Red Cross. She was living at home at first, but she and her dad were having all kinds of difficulties. Then Lucille moved from there and was staying with her girlfriend, Dorothy Harding. She was at Dorothy's when Jimmy started coming, and they had to rush her to the hospital.

There was a problem getting my pay home to Lucille and Jimmy. I had an allotment made out to her, but all the red tape got in the way. The government took such a long time getting things to her, because when she did get the money, she got a pretty big lump sum at one time.

On top of that, things just got wild. Of course, I wasn't even born during the first World War, but I had heard of guys talking about how it was as hard on the wife at home as it was for the man away in the service. Lucille held out a good long while, I guess, before she started running around with her girlfriends and other men.

Sometimes my letters to Lucille were returned by the post office. Every time I got a letter from her, it was from a different return address. Sometimes it was just a post office number. And then I found out that Jimmy wasn't with her. A friend of ours, Freddie Mae Hurd, told me that Mrs. Jeter had Jimmy for a while. What happened was Lucille had brought Jimmy over to her mother's place in the wintertime, and Jimmy didn't have any socks or shoes on. His grandmother was so afraid for his health, she began taking care of him.

Dolores told me about Lucille's carryings-on and that Jimmy was here and there. Lucille just went on a rampage. She bounced around a lot, and I don't know exactly when she got separated from Jimmy. I don't think there was anybody in the Jeter family who was able to take care of Jimmy full-time, since Dolores had started having kids.

I finally got a letter from a stranger, Mrs. Walls, who told me that she had Jimmy and was taking care of him. She worked at Boeing. Mrs. Walls told me that when I got out of the service, I could come and get him there at her place. Lucille was still getting her allotment at that time, but she wasn't paying for Jimmy. So I started sending money to Mrs. Walls, who didn't know where Lucille was half the time.

Unfortunately Mrs. Walls died, and her sister, Mrs. Champ, came up from Berkeley, California, to take care of her sister's affairs, and then she took Jimmy back to Berkeley with her. Later on I got a letter from Mrs. Champ, who told me about her sister dying. She wrote that she had Jimmy and that she would take care of him. I'd never heard of Mrs. Champ before I got this letter. I said, "Well, okay." I was glad that Jimmy finally got settled in one definite place where he would be when I came out. I started divorce proceedings while I was still in the service. Lucille wasn't taking care of Jimmy, so I was just going to end it there.

I was in New Guinea when the news came that the war was over. We already knew it was winding down, and I'd made bets with the guys. I said, "The Germans will surrender before the Japanese." The Germans were trying to fight back at the Battle of the Bulge, but I knew there was no way, that it was futile. And I knew the Japanese were going to fight right down to the wire. I won the bet, but of course I didn't get any money out of it.

I was so happy that the war was over! They began sending the guys home according to how many points they had. You'd get so many points for each kid you had. The more kids you had, the quicker you got home. It made me laugh about one guy there. His wife had twins, and he *knew* they weren't his because he wasn't even there! Of course, his wife wanted to put

My first view of
Seattle after the war—
Smith Tower.

over there."

The guy said, "What?!
I'd dive over the side and
swim home."

"No," I said. "I've
made it this far."

I got my discharge at
Fort Lewis. I didn't know
where Lucille was, but I was
glad to be getting home and
finally seeing Jimmy.

I came back to Seattle in
September 1945. At first I was staying
at my sister-in-law Dolores' place. I was
going to get another place, but then she said,
"You might as well stay here because you're
going to get Jimmy."

I called my mother and sister in Vancouver
to tell them that I was back. My sister sent me a
telegram that said, "Come up here—there's an
emergency." I had told them that I was going to
get Jimmy and then come up there, but they
wanted me to come up there first. I didn't
know if somebody was sick—I thought it might
be my mother—and so I went up there and
found that they were glad I was home and just
wanted to see me. I stayed there for two or
three days, and then I told them, "I'm anxious
to get Jimmy. I've never seen him, and the
people who have him know I'm out of the service." They understood that. So after I got back
from Vancouver I went down to Berkeley. ❧

them on his allotment to get that extra money.
I said, "At least it'll come in handy for you
getting home. Give you some extra points."

He said, "Yeah. I'll give her some extra
points too!"

We were supposed to go to San Francisco,
where I'd get my discharge. I knew Jimmy was
in Berkeley, so I thought to myself, "I'll get
Jimmy and maybe see what's going on in San
Francisco and live there awhile." But as it
turned out the day we were supposed to get to
San Francisco, there was a big Navy celebration
going on. The bay was filled up with Navy
ships, so they sent our ship up to Seattle.

When the ship came in at Elliott Bay, I could
see the old Smith's Tower, a big landmark. I
said to one of the fellows, "Yeah, I live right

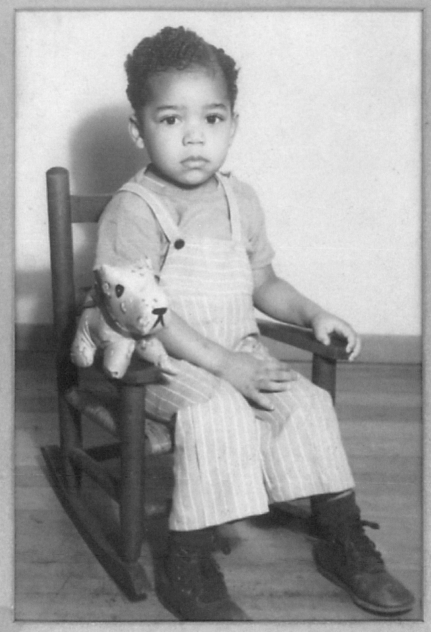

Jimmy Hendrix
age 3 yrs
Taken Jan 15-1946

46

THE FIRST TIME I laid eyes upon Jimmy was when I picked him up in Berkeley. He was living in a project with the Champ family. Mrs. Champ wasn't married then, but her family was taking real good care of Jimmy. Mrs. Champ was a good woman. She was real Christianfied, and she had a compassionate family. They were Texas folks.

Mrs. Champ had told me that when I got out of the service, I could get my son. Of course, her family wanted to keep him. "No," I told her, "he's what I've been thinking about all these years I was in the service."

Mrs. Champ said, "He's your son. I'm

not going to hold you up or try to take advantage of you or give you any hassle," which she didn't.

I felt nervous as I was walking in to meet Jimmy. I said to myself, "I'm finally getting to see my son." It was a feeling I'd never had before.

The first time I saw him, Jimmy had on a little T-shirt, short pants, and sandals. I thought to myself, "This little feller here—that's my *son!*" He was inside, and when we met they said, "Here's your daddy. We've been talking about your daddy." Jimmy was shy when he saw me—he was always on the shy side. I held out my arms and went over to him and hugged him, and Jimmy hugged me.

It was a strange union. Jimmy wasn't scared or anything. He was just bashful, and I felt the same way. I knew I was going to feel that way the first time I saw my son, especially seeing him so big. A new warm baby would have been different. Here he was, three years old, and he was able to look and judge for himself. You hug each other, but it's still funny, and then after a while you get acquainted and start getting used to each other.

When I looked at Jimmy, I could see a lot of his mother in him. His face resembled Lucille's a good deal, especially his eyes. A lot of people who didn't know his mother saw a lot of me in him, whereas I saw both of us. Some of Jimmy's movements and antics reminded me of his mother too, like the way he rolled his eyes sometimes, and then some of what he did reminded me of myself. His smile was a combination of both of us. Jimmy was pigeon-toed, even when he was older, so he walked just like his mother in that respect.

Of course, Jimmy didn't know *me*, actually, but the Champs had told him that his daddy was coming to get him, and they had a picture of me in my uniform there on the table. He knew that picture was dad. After we hugged, Jimmy and I were sitting there talking, and

Mrs. Champ's daughter, Celestine, asked him, "Where's your daddy?"

Both were there at the same time! Jimmy pointed at the picture. "There's daddy."

"No," she said, pointing at me, "there's your daddy there."

Jimmy looked at me and said, "That's not daddy." He was a little confused because he knew that picture as daddy.

Celestine said, "Yeah, this is your dad now."

So Jimmy just sat there and looked at me as though he were thinking, "This is it? Yeah, okay." I know it was strange for Jimmy. More than anything, though, I just sat there and looked at him and thought, "Hey! This is my son!"

I'd come down on the train with just my bag, and I stayed with Mrs. Champ's family about a week before we left. I mostly stuck around the projects and got acquainted with Jimmy. He had a little playmate next door who came over every once in a while, and before I got there Jimmy wanted to call that boy's father "dad" too, because of that little boy calling him dad. But Mrs. Champ had told him, "That's not your daddy. Your daddy's in the army." While we were there, Jimmy liked to ride around on that little boy's tricycle. Mrs. Champ's son was fond of Jimmy too, and he didn't want to go to the station to see us off because he didn't want to see Jimmy leave.

When I brought Jimmy back on the train, he started playing with a little kid, running up and down the aisles. This little kid, who might have been a little bit older than Jimmy, came up to me and said, "Yeah, I enjoy playing with him, even if he is *Chinese!*"

I had to take another look at Jimmy! Then I had to laugh.

I gave Jimmy his first spanking on that train. I guess he got a little homesick, and he misbehaved. I said, "No. Don't do that."

He was going to keep doing it anyway, so I said, "Here's where the show's over." It was at

night and people were sleeping in their seats in the coach, so I took Jimmy in between the cars, where the car coupling was, and closed the door. People wouldn't be able to hear all that much noise because of the clacking of the wheels. I said, "Are you going to behave?" as I whacked him on the bottom a few times.

Jimmy yelled, "Celestine! Celestine!"

I said, "Celestine's way back there."

"Where's Celestine?"

"She's back there in Berkeley." After that he simmered down.

When I punished Jimmy after that, he just took it in stride. He'd say he wouldn't do it any more. He knew that I'd only repeat something so many times: "Okay, now simmer down. If I have to say it one more time, I'm coming after you." After that it was too late. For me it was like that old saying, "Hurts me more than it hurts you." I'd prefer to use reason and talk to him: "I just don't want you to do what you're doing. You're going to harm yourself, and it's just wrong anyhow."

I kept in touch with Mrs. Champ and her family for a while, and then I got so busy we lost contact. I'm sorry about that. I've thought about them so many times and wondered where they're at. I don't think Jimmy ever had contact with those people again either, but he remembered Mrs. Champ after he grew up. They were a good family. I know that they would have probably raised Jimmy really good.

❧   ❧   ❧

AFTER I BROUGHT Jimmy back from California, I had his name legally changed. Lucille had given our baby the name Johnny Allen, which could've been the name of some guy she might've been running around with while I was overseas—that's the only way I look at it. I wanted to call him "Jimmy" because my first name is James, so I named him James

Marshall Hendrix. That's what's on his birth certificate, and there's a little asterisk that says his name was changed from Johnny Allen.

But I didn't start calling him Jimmy then. When he was really young, we all called him "Buster." That was a name his Aunt Dolores gave him when he was born. She said, "Whoa, he was a buster," because he was so big. We were still calling him Buster until he was around five or six. Finally he said to me, "Dad, I want to be named Jimmy. I don't want to be Buster anymore."

"Oh? Why?"

"Well, they all call me Buster Brown at school."

"I understand that," I told Jimmy, "and after all it's just a nickname. Okay, from here after, you're just called Jimmy or James."

When I brought Jimmy back to Seattle, we stayed with Lucille's sister Dolores at a little house on Jackson Street—it's not there anymore. I was going to get an apartment, but she was doing some night work and she said, "You might as well stay here. Lucille will be showing up eventually, and you can say what you have to say."

On top of that, Dolores had at least two kids—Roberta and Julia—and she may have had her third one, Dee Dee, by then. This was all a surprise to me, because when I left she didn't have any, although while I was overseas she'd sent me a picture of Jimmy and Roberta laying on a blanket together. Jimmy was older than any of Dolores' daughters, and I could take care of all the kids while she worked. It was a small house, two or three bedrooms. We didn't live there very long, though, because Dolores was in the process of getting a place at Yesler Terrace. When she did, Jimmy and I moved in there with her.

MY DAD SMOKED A PIPE, SO I THOUGHT I'D TRY ONE.

Yesler Terrace was a permanent project. It was well built, because the places are still there, and it has always been racially integrated. I think our unit was number 577 or 579. It was part of a long wooden building. There was a fenced-in back yard where Jimmy could play, and the people next door could use it too.

A lot of the early pictures of Jimmy were taken in that apartment, like the picture of Jimmy sitting on my knee and the picture of me with a pipe. There was also a picture taken of Jimmy and Lucille, which I gave to Dolores.

We were all living together on Yesler Way when Lucille showed up. Jimmy and I had gone by to visit an elderly woman who was an old friend of the Jeter family from way back. As a matter of fact, she raised Dolores after she got to a certain age. The Jeters called her "Mama Hankins," and I did too. She told Lucille that I was back, and not long after that Lucille came knocking on her sister's door and said, "Here I am."

I hadn't seen Lucille since I went in the service, and she'd changed. She'd sent me a picture of herself with Jimmy, where she still looked real young, like a teenager. Now she was more grown up, and she had this wild, independent air about her. She was altogether different, and of course I figured she'd be that way. She was docile and on the timid side when I left, and she had an innocent look. Now she'd been around. She looked more experienced.

At first Lucille acted skittish, holding her head down like a kid who has to stand in front of her parent. She knew she did a lot of bad things, and she was trying to figure out how I was going to take it. She wanted to know if I was going to blow up, but I said, "No."

I asked Lucille about her not taking care of Jimmy, and she said, "Well, I was moving around so much."

My feelings were lukewarm, but I was still attracted to her. I thought, "I was gone so long, and she was so young when I left."

I knew all along that it was not going to be the same when I got back. That was one thing I hated when I went in the army, because I'd told myself I'd never get in that position. I'd heard some guys from the first World War talk about how when they came back after the war their wives were wild and woolly. I'd always said, "I'm not going to get married and go in the service," but then it happened to me.

The divorce I started getting while I was in the service was going to cost me seventy-five dollars, and I had one more payment to make. I was going to send it in, but then Lucille said, "Do you want to try to make it?"

"Okay," I said. "I know how it was, me being away. Maybe the best thing to do is to give it a bloody go again." So that's what I did. We started right from there.

Jimmy gave Lucille the same treatment he gave me when we first met. He hadn't seen her since she left him with Mrs. Champ's sister, so she was a stranger to him too. By that time, though, he was used to me and being around Dolores and her kids.

Lucille went down to the main post office to get her final allotment, and we bought some clothes with it. I paid that divorce attorney after I called him and told him that we were going to reconcile. I got my bonus from the service too—they called it "52/20." For fifty-two weeks after your discharge, you'd get twenty dollars a week. Of course, nowadays that would go nowhere, and even back in '45 it would run low. But you could still get a meal in some restaurants for twenty-five cents. A lot of times I'd go down to skid row, where I could get a bowl of beans for ten cents and stew for fifteen cents. It was filling.

Not long after I got out of the army, I tried to take Jimmy and Lucille up to Vancouver, but I had trouble with customs. We were going on

Jimmy, 1946.

52

"Hell," I said, "I done been in the service as an American citizen!"

Anyway, they had it all screwed around, so we stayed all night in a shed at the immigration office and then took the bus back to Seattle. After I got that all straightened out, we went up there again and stayed at the same house I'd lived in with Mr. Moore. This was the first time my mom met Lucille, and she liked her. Lucille liked my mother too. This was also the first time Jimmy met my mom, and he enjoyed having another grandma. My mom did different little things to make him feel special, like asking if he wanted to eat this and that. She liked being a grandma and took it all in stride.

We had dinner with Harry Hastings' folks. I'd tried to keep in touch with Harry after I left Vancouver the first time, and I'd heard from him when I was in the service. I'd sent him a carton of Lucky Strikes because he was in the Canadian army and Lucky Strikes were hard to get. But he wasn't home yet, and I didn't get to see Harry again after that. Later on down the road I heard that he'd died. The Onos were gone because they'd been put in an internment camp. I don't know what became of Maso's brothers and sisters after they were sent to the camp, and I never saw Maso after that. My mother told me she saw Maso one time after the war and talked with him.

the bus, because I didn't have a car. When we got to the border, the customs agent asked us where we were born. With Jimmy and his mother, everything was okay. When they asked me, I said, "I was born in Vancouver, B.C."

They said, "We've got to check that out," so we had to get off the bus.

"We could let you through," one of the agents said, "but you might have trouble getting back."

When we returned home, Lucille and I got along at first. We stayed at her sister's place in Yesler Terrace for a while and baby-sat when Dolores worked at night. But Lucille and her sister didn't get along too well. They'd have fights every once in a while, so Jimmy, Lucille, and I moved to the Golden Hotel on Tenth Avenue. This was a real scroungy transient hotel that was off the beaten path, right around where the prostitutes were. We only had one small room for all three of us—one bed, one chair, a table, and a gas hot plate. There was no refrigerator, so we'd put items in a box outside the window to try to keep them cool. In the winter that was okay, but in the summertime there was no way of keeping milk or butter or anything perishable out there overnight. The lavatory and bath were down the hall, and Jimmy, Lucille, and I all had to sleep in the same bed.

I started working at Fry's Packing House, sacking bone meal and doing whatever chores needed doing. I never did go up on the killing floor, though, because I didn't want to see them hit the cows and pigs on the head with a hammer. The people who ran the place would go down to First Avenue and get a bunch of transients to come in and do the killing and shake the hides. They'd give them slickers to wear, but it was still a messy job, and I'm glad I didn't have to do that.

Mrs. Champ sent me an army footlocker with a lot of nice little clothes in it for Jimmy. They were all washed and starched. There were all kinds of little toys and goodies in there. I've still got that footlocker. Jimmy didn't get a chance to wear a lot of the clothes, though, because they got stolen not long after they arrived.

I wasn't making much money at Fry's, so I thought about working with the merchant marines. I didn't like the idea of taking a ship —I always said, "Not for no married man!"— but we needed the money, so I started going down to the union halls. There were two of them—the Marine Cooks and Stewards, and the N.M.U., which was the National Maritime Union. I never shipped out with the Marine Cooks and Stewards. The N.M.U., people said, was associated with the communists. They had parties with racially mixed couples

and so on, and I used to go to these parties just to be sociable. Because of this, I had a run-in with the government when I was applying for my seaman's license. The people at the maritime board thought I might be "a threat to national security."

When I met with the board, a bunch of people were sitting around, and someone said, "Why did you go to those N.M.U. parties?"

I said, "They're social events, and there isn't any prejudice. They believe that everybody is equal."

One of the government men asked, "Don't you think that bringing about desegregation will take a little time?"

I told him, "It's been going on like this for so long, I think it should be done *now*. People are just putting it off, putting it off. When? When will it happen? There ought to be a date set or get it done now."

The board looked skeptical. The man said, "That takes some time."

"Yeah, all these hundreds of years it's been going on, and they're still dragging their feet."

I did get my card, and I got on a merchant marine Victory ship called the *Marshall.* We went over to Yokohama to bring troops back from Japan. I had a nice job on the ship. I made the bunks and took care of the passenger cabins. It was easy. I got my job done early—actually, around twelve o'clock—and I was through for the rest of the day.

❧   ❧   ❧

JAPAN WAS DEVASTATED when I got there in 1946. Before we went ashore, we watched the stevedores unloading the ship. They were Japanese veterans, and some of them still wore their army hats. I felt so sorry for them because they were so hungry. After we had our lunch one day, the cook set out some of the leftover food in a big metal pan for these stevedores. Man, they just got into it. I said, "These people are starving!"

The captain told the cook not to do it again. The cook said, "I felt sorry for them—they're so hungry."

"No," the captain told him, "the government doesn't want us to be feeding them."

While we were looking over the side of the ship, one of the seamen was eating an apple. He threw the core down on the dock, and one of the stevedores grabbed it and chomped on it. We said, "Damn!" I just felt a whole lot of compassion for those people.

The MPs had to frisk us to make sure we weren't taking anything ashore. They didn't allow us to take any American money or any more cigarettes than we'd use ourselves, because some of the guys would sell cigarettes on the black market. I did that myself. We'd put a carton down our backs. Some of the MPs were okay—they'd let you go on through—and other guys were real hard-nosed about frisking you. So we'd always find out which were the good guys.

After we'd get past the MPs, there'd be all these girls standing around saying, "Ooh, come with me" and "Trick or treat." Some guys would have one on each arm. I said, "No. I want to get to town to see what's up there."

Yokohama was so devastated. It was all bombed out. As I walked around, I could see where buildings had been. There were little kids wandering around with satchels on their shoulders. Most of the people didn't seem to be all haggard and moping around, though. They seemed to be thinking about survival. On the voyage back, the troops were sure glad to be going home.

I was gone about two weeks, and while I was away, Mrs. Jeter took a trip to Kansas to see her sister. She wanted to take Jimmy, and Lucille let him go along. After I arrived, I went up to my room at the Golden Hotel, and the place was locked up. I asked the manager about it, and he told me, "Oh, yeah. Lucille got put out."

"What? What about all the clothes and that?"

"Yeah, that was put out in the street, and that stuff is gone."

I'd left my army uniform there, and the only clothes I had left were just what I had taken with me to Japan, and I didn't take a whole lot. I said, "Oh, damn." Jimmy was gone with his grandmother when this happened.

I asked around and found out that some guy came by there, and Lucille and this guy were caught up there in the room together and all that old stuff. So the landlady put her out. I found out where some of the stuff was and visited those places. I went to one woman's house, and I could see her little kid playing with Jimmy's toys. I thought, "Well, I'll just let him have those." I could see Jimmy's footlocker too, so I asked about the footlocker and the clothes. The lady said, "I don't know a thing about that."

I said, "Well, that's my son's footlocker." So I got the footlocker, but I don't know where my uniform went.

I was angry, missing my clothes, and I didn't know where Lucille was. She'd just taken off somewhere, and so I went by Mama Hankins' place. She had been in contact with Mrs. Jeter, and Mrs. Jeter was saying something about needing some money to come home from Kansas. I said, "Oh, boy, all this stuff is falling on me."

Mrs. Hankins said, "Here's fifty dollars, Al. Keep it."

"No."

She said, "Yeah. You can pay me whenever you can." I talked to Mrs. Jeter on the phone and told her that Lucille wasn't around. She said, "She was there when Jimmy left." I sent the money to Mrs. Jeter, and she came back with Jimmy. Dolores found out about all this, so she told me to come back to her place with Jimmy. A little while later Lucille and I got back together, and we all stayed with Dolores until we got a place of our own at the Rainier Vista housing project in 1947.

≈ ≈ ≈

RAINIER VISTA was a nice place in the Rainier Valley. It was a permanent housing project that was built before the war, and it was more elaborate than Yesler Terrace, which was over in town. Rainier Vista had a lot more well-kept lawns, and it was real quiet. There was a lot of greenery around. All the places were one-story, and in each building there were one, two, or three units, and some of the units had two or three bedrooms. The first place Lucille, Jimmy, and I moved to was a one-bedroom unit at 3121 Oregon Street. We were on one end of the building, and another couple was on the other end. It was a nice place that's still there.

The first piece of furniture Lucille and I got was one of those davenport couches that you could stretch out and make into another bed. We had it in the front room. That couch cost ninety dollars, and I bought it on time—I put so much down and had to pay so much a month. Then I got some of that nude furniture—you could get that pretty cheap—and painted it.

Our first place had a large closet space. Jimmy's crib-type bed fit in there just nice, so he slept in the closet. He'd go in there while Lucille and I were fighting too. When it came to tempers, Lucille and I were about equalized, and she'd get mad and bang things around. Jimmy knew the hardship. He was old enough to see all the hassles we were having.

When she was on her good behavior, though, Lucille did really good with Jimmy. She'd be cuddling him and talking to him, and he'd be hugging on her. He was affectionate with his mother. When she'd be busy doing things around the house, he'd be playing with his toys and just doing his thing. He didn't want to be mollycoddled over all the time—he was independent too. I was also affectionate with Jimmy. When he was small, I hugged him and told him that I loved him. When he got a little older, it wasn't "mannish" to hug too much.

I was going to school and working. I started studying electronics under the GI Bill. We had to get by on ninety dollars a month. Our rent was close to forty dollars a month, so I did a lot of extra part-time work at the Pike Place Market. It was a tight squeeze. School let out at three o'clock, and I'd come home, eat, and take the bus to go to work from around five o'clock until twelve. That market was quite a tourist place, and I swept the refuse that farmers left behind. By the time I'd come home, Jimmy would be in bed or getting ready to go to bed. He was scared of the dark sometimes, so we'd leave a light on. He had nightmares a few times, but it wasn't a continuous thing.

It was only on the weekends that we'd get to talking. I could have a little bit of time with Jimmy on Saturday because I didn't have to go to school, but I still worked. On Sundays I could have more time with him. Sometimes I'd roughhouse with him a little bit—nearly all kids like that—and he'd laugh when I'd be tussling him around. Jimmy was ticklish, and he had a good sense of humor. He'd laugh at jokes or when he was making his toys do different things.

Jimmy had a way of being shy when he was meeting people. He was one of those kids who hang around their parents' legs. He'd grab ahold of his mother, and she'd be in the forefront. I'd say, "Come out and speak to Mrs. So-and-so," and he'd keep his finger in his mouth and say, "*Ehhh.*" He just didn't want to say anything because he was too shy to talk, or he'd talk real low and people wouldn't know what he was saying. He also stammered, but it wasn't real bad, like a stutter. When it was just us, Jimmy still wasn't overly talkative, but he asked his share of questions about how and why.

Jimmy liked other children, and he was always around them. There was a little white girl a couple of doors away from us in another unit at Yesler Terrace, and she became Jimmy's playmate. She'd come over and get Jimmy, and they'd run around together. She was a friendly gal, and they'd play in the dirt and make mud pies and yackety-yack. They'd go over to her house too. There weren't any other kids his size around there.

Behind our place on Oregon Street was a cement tennis court and a big grass field where kids would play touch football and soccer. The first school Jimmy ever went to was right at the end of that play field. It wasn't day care, but a preschool baby class. His mother took him the first day, and after that Jimmy would just walk by himself to the school.

Jimmy had an imaginary friend when we lived in Rainier Vista. Once he was doing something that he had no business doing, and I was getting after him. I said, "You know you shouldn't be doing that. Where did you get this from? Who told you to do that?"

He said, "Sessa say."

"'Sessa say'? Who you talking about, 'Sessa say'?"

Jimmy said, "Sessa say."

Jimmy didn't say if Sessa was a he or a she. I said, "Sessa say he's going to get you in trouble, whoever he is!" Jimmy was doing everything Sessa say, and he wouldn't do whatever I'd say! Later on I saw a motion picture where a little kid had an imaginary friend, and they talked him out of that. I said, "Yeah, that's Jimmy!"

because he'd have his imaginary friend sitting there too.

Jimmy always had an imagination playing with his toys. He could play by himself a good while—he'd go in his room with his little cars and trucks. He'd go out in the back yard and get down in the dirt with his little dump truck, going through the motions. Kids don't do that so much now, it seems. They've got their Nintendos and the tube. I guess they've got their imagination, but you just don't see it as much.

JIMMY LIKED HIS AUNT BELLE.

Jimmy had a little stuffed doll that he played with. He also liked crayons, and he'd be coloring up everything. He'd use his imagination making his own toys too. Sometimes he'd sit down and make little imaginary guys out of clothespins the way my brother Frank and I made them. When he was a little older, he'd make toy hydroplanes out of clothespins and paint them. All the kids used to do that— they were crazy about the hydro races in Seattle.

Jimmy played his share of hide-and-seek, and he also shot marbles a little bit. He liked to play war, naturally. He had a toy gun, a cap pistol, out there in Rainier Vista, and toy soldiers too. They didn't have a lot of dinosaur toys in the shops like they do now, but I talked to Jimmy about dinosaurs because I always remembered *The Lost World*, a silent picture my parents took me to see when I was a little kid.

Jimmy liked holidays. He enjoyed going out trick-or-treating on Halloween. We didn't have money to buy outfits, so we'd paint his face up and put a paper hat on his head. He had a sweet tooth, so he liked the candy. Jimmy believed in Santa Claus and liked to decorate the Christmas tree, but he didn't seem to want much when he was little. He was pretty easy to please. He was always thrilled with any kind of toy he got because he didn't get too many of them. I didn't have all that much, and I had to explain the situation to him. He'd be talking about how some kid had more than him, and I'd say, "We can't keep up with the Joneses, as the old saying goes."

I just told him about the way it was when I was coming up: "You just couldn't get what Tommy Jones across the street got. Maybe both of Tommy Jones' parents work, and their income's different. The main thing is having a roof over your head, some food in your stomach, and getting your bills paid, and then you go from there. Don't be going overboard just for show or a lot of unnecessaries." When I was a kid, there were a lot of times where I said, "Gee, I wish for this," and my mom would say, "Yeah, I'd like to have such-and-such too—if we could get it." After my dad died, things got so tight, I'd tell her, "Don't get me any presents for Christmas. I just want some food, and that's all."

We had birthday parties for Jimmy when he was small, but later on I'd mostly just kind of pass his birthday up. I'd give him something, but as far as parties go, I didn't do much. I never did have a birthday party myself until I was grown up. Eventually, my second wife's kids used to come by and surprise me with gifts. I said, "Wow! If you live to be an old man, then you can have a birthday party."

Jimmy was born left-handed, but I encouraged him to do things right-handed. When he was sitting at the table when he was a little kid and he'd be eating with his fork or spoon in his left hand, I'd put it in his right hand. And so he became right-handed in writing and eating. Jimmy did everything just like an ordinary,

conventional right-handed person would do, except playing baseball. He batted left-handed, although he pitched right-handed. In his teens he started playing guitar right-handed at first, but found that he could play left-handed easier.

When he was little Jimmy was already showing an interest in music. He would usually pat his foot to music or bang on pans. Then I gave him a couple of sticks and a box to beat on instead of on the pans, because he'd knock dents in them. I also made him a little guitar-like instrument out of a cigar box. I cut a hole in the top and sealed the lid to keep it from flopping open, and then I pasted on a wood neck and used elastic bands for strings. He couldn't get a whole lot of music out of it, but it was a great imaginary piece, and he played with that. Jimmy never messed around with a violin as a kid, like some authors have written, but he did have a ukulele that I found while cleaning out somebody's basement. I fixed it up and got some strings for it. The ukulele only has four strings, and it's more of a chord-type instrument. Back then you'd sing with them, and people used to take ukuleles to picnics.

Jimmy had a harmonica when he was small, but he didn't know how to play it. All of us had harmonicas when we were kids. I'd go "whoo, whoo," blowing whistles in and out, but I never did learn how to play harmonica. And it was about the same way with Jimmy. He might have learned a little more than I did, but I never heard him play songs on the harmonica.

When Jimmy was around four or five, I got him a pair of roller skates. In my teens, I was crazy about skating. But the first time Jimmy fell on his back, that killed it with the skates. He didn't want to get on them anymore.

I always wanted to take Jimmy swimming because I love to swim. The first time Lucille and I took him to the beach, he had a suit on and walked right on into the water. I said, "Ooh, wow." This was at Lake Washington, where there's no tides and hardly any waves at all unless a boat goes by. But it was a little choppy that day, and Jimmy was just walking along like there was nothing to it. A wave hit him and knocked him down, and Jimmy gulped some water. He turned around and came out, and I couldn't get him back in again. I told Lucille, "They say not to force a person— otherwise you'll make them really scared." Another time Jimmy, Lucille, her mother, and I went swimming at Madrona Beach.

Jimmy liked going to the park. Lucille and I would take him to Seward Park, where they had swings and slides and a sandbox. I showed Jimmy how to swing himself, so he could start off pumping and do his own swinging. Of course sometimes he'd get lazy and want me to push him. He'd go on a merry-go-round where the kids would run on the outside to get the thing going and then hop on it. We would also have picnics at Leschi Park. Sometimes Jimmy would try to catch bees in a jar, and he'd get stung. I told him, "That's the reason why them bees are stinging you—they don't want to be made prisoners." He wanted them to show to the other kids.

My Aunt Belle came to stay with us for a while when Lucille and I were still together. She still had a lot of showmanship in her, and she entertained us with her singing and danc- ing. Belle had a son and a daughter, and her daughter was into entertainment too—she used to sing and dance. Jimmy liked Aunt Belle, but he was too young to realize who she was. She was just another visitor as far as he was con- cerned. Afterwards, Belle went to Vancouver to see my mother, and they had a fine time. It had been years since they'd seen each other. They always kept in touch by mail, but to see each other in person was so special for them. Belle lived in New York, and after that visit we always kept in contact by mail. We'd write her all the time, but she just visited us that one time.

LUCILLE HAD a good sense of humor. She was easy to make friends with, and she had her fill of phone talk with the gals. One time I was in the background singing while Lucille was talking on the telephone, and the other person asked her who was on the radio. She said, "Oh, no, that's Al singing. That's all I can tell you." The other person never did believe her, and Lucille had a laugh about that.

Lucille loved to party, and if there was any booze in the house, it wouldn't be there long. I could bring a couple of cans of beer to drink right away, but I wasn't that much of a drinker, and I sure ain't a lush! Usually when Lucille and I had alcohol at the house, we drank together, and there'd be other people there too, so it was a party. Lucille liked being the life of the party, and the alcohol provided some stimulant for that. Sometimes we'd go to a dance or some- body else's house, and she'd get loaded.

It was almost like a cycle. Things would go along real nice for two or three months. After that I'd go, "Uh-oh. Things are going too smooth. I hate to think about it, but some- thing's going to happen." I'd get that old gut feeling, and sure enough, something would be up.

Lucille's mother came over a lot because she was crazy about Jimmy. After all, he was her first grandchild. She'd stay for two or three days. That was okay, but I always knew that as long as her mother was there, Lucille was liable to take off any old time, since somebody was looking after Jimmy.

One time I came home from school and she was gone. I asked her mother, "Where's Lucille?"

"Oh, she went to the store."

My wife, Lucille.

Lucille Hendrix

1948

"How long ago was that?"

"Oh, that was around two o'clock."

Heck, the store was just down the street. She still didn't come back during the time I was eating and getting ready for my night job at the Pike Place Market. I said, "Oh, sheesh! Dadgummit, she done gone to town or stopped by to yackety-yack with some of her girlfriends out there in the projects."

I called her girlfriends, and they hadn't seen her. I said, "Uh-huh."

At the time, we were living from one check to the next, stretching and holding on. I checked the drawer where I kept all the money, and Lucille had grabbed the last twenty dollars. She'd taken off, gone downtown goofing around. I said, "Hell!" I figured she was fooling around with another guy.

A lot of that went on for a while. I wouldn't see her for a couple of days, and then she'd call up and say, "I'm down at so-and-so's."

"Yeah," I'd tell her. "You just cut out and disappear."

Jimmy wasn't able to hide his feelings about all this. His emotions came out real easy in his face and his eyes. He'd get upset and ask, "Where's mom at?"

I'd say, "I don't know."

I'm not overly jealous, but with the things Lucille did, a lot of guys would say, "Man, you sure can take it." They'd tell me that they'd blow her away.

"No," I'd tell them. "I ain't going to do anything of that sort. You're given too long of a time to sit in that cell and say, 'Oh, why in the hell did I do it?' and wish you hadn't. I'm going to weigh the consequences."

I never bopped Lucille around, because I don't believe in fighting like that. One guy I knew used to get at it with his wife, and he'd call me up and say, "Give her a little brushing up when you come in. Bop 'em around a little bit, even if they haven't done anything. Get one ahead of them and tell them that's in case

you do do something." But I didn't believe in that. When I got mad at Lucille, I'd just give her a tongue-lashing. I wouldn't cuss her out, but I'd say, "You know what you're supposed to do, and you don't want to do it!"

I got in a lot of embarrassing spots with her, and I just didn't say anything. I'm quite sure Jimmy was aware that Lucille was running around, and it must have affected him.

Sometimes Lucille and I would be arguing, and Lucille's mother would ask me, "Why don't you stay home and watch to see what happens?"

"I can't do that!" I told her. "What are you talking about? Somebody's got to make some money." I was the only breadwinner. Lucille didn't have to work the whole time we were together. I went to school in the daytime under the GI Bill and worked at night for five years.

Of course, whenever Lucille took off, Jimmy's grandmother would be there with him. Mrs. Jeter took real good care of him. She'd feed him and do special things to keep him from getting into mischief. But the situation with Lucille always felt like a time bomb.

Things got even rougher after I found out she was pregnant again. Lucille and I were still together when her second son, Leon, was born on January 13, 1948, but I knew he wasn't mine. Before Leon was born, Lucille had started living with a Filipino man named Frank. She always said she planned to come back home, but she just wanted to stay with Frank for a while. She was there a month or so and then came back. While she was staying there, I had to go see her at Frank's place if I needed to talk to her about something. During this time, Lucille's mother was usually staying at my place and taking care of Jimmy, and I was there taking care of him at night.

As soon as Leon was born, Lucille and I could both see that he was Frank's son, not mine. He had a sort of Asian look, with real straight hair. Lucille had to admit that Leon was Frank's son. So Leon and Jimmy had the same mother, but Jimmy is my only child. I've never told Leon straight out about who his dad is, although he has asked me. I think he halfway knows the truth because he heard it from his Aunt Dolores. But I always told him, "Just forget about it."

I haven't seen Leon's dad for a long time now, but at the time I said to him, "What are you going to do about it? Are you going to take care of the baby?" He just shrugged his shoulders and got a silly look on his face. I used to imitate him and Lucille would laugh. I think later on Jimmy was aware that Leon wasn't his full brother. I never did tell him directly, but Jimmy felt it.

While Lucille was having the affair with Frank, I just thought, "She's going to do what she's going to do anyhow, so . . ." But I never had another woman on the side, because I was too busy taking care of the family. Just because Lucille was doing it, I wasn't going to. I believe in fidelity in marriage.

Lucille did have some good points, though. She was very affectionate with the kids. She could be a good housewife and mother for a while. When she buckled down and took care of the kids, she did okay. We agreed on one thing If the boys did something wrong, she'd say, "Your dad's going to getcha when he gets home."

Lucille would spank them sometimes too, and she wouldn't let them act up, especially in public. Some kids will pull a tantrum and lay down and kick and scream. The mother's standing there saying, "Johnny, you get up and behave yourself," and the kid's just screaming. Lucille wouldn't let Jimmy or Leon do anything like that, so we agreed in that respect. I'd tell her, "That's one thing I can't stand. Your parents didn't let you do it, and there ain't no sense in letting the kids do it either."

She'd say, "No, they ain't going to act up like that."

The same year Leon was born, Lucille's next son, Joey, started coming along. My wife told me that Joey wasn't mine, but like Leon he also used the last name of Hendrix. I hate to mention the name of Joey's dad, because I don't know if the guy knows he's the father. He was a close friend who had a lot of leisure time from his job, and he'd come around when I'd be out working. He had a big Oldsmobile and we didn't have any transportation, so he'd tell both of us, "Any time you want to go anywhere, just call me." And he made that offer specific with Lucille.

After Lucille had Joey we got a two-bedroom unit at 3022 Genesee Street in the Rainier Vista projects. Jimmy and Leon had one room, while Joey stayed in a bassinet in the room with Lucille and me. I was studying hard for school, and sometimes I'd be home at night doing my homework with the kids. I'd be humming and rocking Leon in the cradle with my foot and working the slide rule, all at the same time.

After Joey was born, things got hectic. I'd come home and it'd seem like he hadn't eaten anything. Lucille would say, "No, I fed him." I found out later on that he wasn't getting the proper care and was suffering from malnutrition. I thought, "What the heck's going on?" I had to send him to a woman who had a special way of taking care of kids who were suffering and needed a lot of special care. We also found out that his feet needed adjusting, so I had to take him to get special fitted shoes that cost a bundle. I wasn't hardly doing any work then, so it was hard.

For a while I just went on with things the way they were. I went to work when I had to, and I did my homework. I said, "I just have to live with it and wait until Lucille decides to stay or go."

While I was going through my troubles with Lucille, there was an old fellow at the Pike Place Market, Dad Carr, and I'd sit and talk with him. He'd console me. I wouldn't be crying on his shoulder, but I'd say, "Yeah, she's

size of that." I just wanted to see that they'd be taken care of.

I can't fathom anybody neglecting their children or disregarding them. A parent should be a child's best friend and raise him right and teach him all the right things. A parent has to be consistent with things like discipline—every day—and that responsibility lasts all your life. Parents owe their child a great deal because, after all, they're the cause of the child being there. I knew that being a single parent was going to be a hassle—you have to mend and wash and iron the clothes, cook, clean, go to work, and do everything else without much time off for yourself. But if you have children, you're supposed to take care of them.

Lucille talked about trying to contest the divorce, but she didn't put up too much of a fight. I said, "You can contest all you want," but she never did. It was an open-and-shut case. She didn't even show up at the courthouse, so I got custody of the kids. Lucille moved out, and I think she got on welfare. I know she wasn't going to receive any support from me because I had the kids.

After the divorce, Jimmy and Leon never went to stay with their mother. She wanted to be around the kids, but she wanted her freedom too. It was like that old saying, "You can't have your cake and eat it too." Jimmy was

doin' this and doin' that."

He'd tell me, "That's life. You just have to grin and bear it or do something about it."

I finally divorced Lucille when I'd had enough. That was around 1950, when Leon was two. At the time Lucille was doing a lot of running around with Jerry Monroe, this underage little guy who used to baby-sit Jimmy. I said, "This is it."

Once I made up my mind to get divorced, I told Lucille, "What the heck, I'm going to get the kids because I know they'll be well taken care of. The way it is right now, if they went with you, they probably wouldn't even see any part of my child support. You're going off, leaving them with your mother, so I know the around his mother most of the time when we were still together, but after the divorce he was just around me.

I adopted Joey out when things got too rough for us. I was out of work at the time, and later on Leon had to go to a foster home too. Jimmy was the only one to stick with me. He was the oldest, and the adoption people told me I had to sign Joey away because he needed a lot of extra help. They also said that once I signed the papers, I wasn't supposed to make any contact with him, and that's what I always went by. When Joey was adopted, they used the Hendrix name, but I saw something one time where the last part of his name was spelled differently.

Jimmy never got to know Joey when he was older, but he knew of him. After he formed the Experience, Jimmy asked me if I ever saw Joey. I told him, "Occasionally I've seen him, though I wasn't allowed to talk to him because that was in the ruling when I adopted him out." The last time Jimmy saw Joey was when he was small, and Jimmy was still rather small himself.

Lucille had two daughters after we broke up, and they didn't use the Hendrix name. I don't know what last name Lucille gave them, but Jerry Monroe is their father. At one time Jerry's mother lived right up the street from Lucille and me at Rainier Vista. Jerry was still a teenager when he got Lucille pregnant, and boy, his mother had a fit.

I'm sure that Jimmy's half-sisters are still alive. The first child, Cathleen, was born practically blind, although they didn't know that until she was at least a year old. The other one, Pam, was okay. Lucille and I were on a talking basis when she had her, and I'd go by there and play with her in the crib. I called her Miss Pam. I could see some of the characteristics of Lucille and Jerry Monroe's mother in her.

Years later I saw Pam across the street from my house. Before I knew who she was, I said to my second wife, "You know, she reminds me

of somebody I knew in the past—her antics, the way she sits and talks, and some of the other motions she makes." An elderly couple were taking care of her, and they just looked too old to have had the child themselves.

Later on I was doing some yard work for them, and the father said, "Oh, yeah, we adopted Pam." That's as far as our conversation went, but it just came to me then: "Doggone, now I know who she is! That's Lucille's daughter, Pam." That was so surprising. I remembered Pam from when she was a little kid, and the way she carried on and talked was just like her grandmother on her dad's side.

The first or second time that Jimmy came to Seattle as the Experience, he was at the house and Pam came over and wanted to get his autograph. At that time I didn't know she was Lucille's daughter—it wasn't until two or three years later that I found out who she was—but I said, "Yeah, okay, you can come on in."

I introduced her to Jimmy and told him about her wanting an autograph, and so he gave her one. I don't know what he wrote, but she was very pleased. And then when I found out about who Pam was, I thought, "Damn, here she was getting her brother's autograph!"

Later on Pam was working as a nurse's aide at a hospital, and one of the patients who had been an old resident of Seattle started talking to her and found out about her background. He said, "I think your mother was Lucille Jeter." One word led to another, and then Pam called me and said, "Mr. Hendrix, have I got something interesting to tell you!"

She went on to tell me about how this person had told her about her birth, and I said, "Yeah." I didn't relate to her the story about how her antics reminded me of Jerry Monroe's mother. I thought, "Man, this is like one of those fantastic stories." Dolores Jeter told me that Lucille's other daughter, Cathleen, was making brooms at a blind school. She may also be aware that Jimmy is her half-brother.

Lucille was a good-looking gal when we split up, and she was still looking good after she had Pam. Later on down the road, Lucille had another boy, and after that she was looking pretty rough. I know she called him Alfred. I only saw him twice, when he was an infant. I asked her who fathered him, and I don't think she knew. I knew the guy she was going with at the time—his name was Al—and I said, "Oh, this is Al's baby?"

She said, "No, it's not his. You don't know who the father is." Then she just laughed. That's all I know about Alfred, and today he probably doesn't even know what's up. I have no idea where Cathleen, Pam, and Alfred are today, although some of them might bear a physical resemblance to Jimmy through their mother.

I believe Joey is still alive. When he was a kid, I'd see him riding his bike around the Central Area. Years later when I was living in the Queen Anne district, Joey was working at the same place as Leon, making signs for the city. Leon didn't let Joey know that he was his half-brother—I don't know why—but Leon was saying, "Yeah, he's a good worker. He's smart."

"Yeah!" I said to Leon. "He's doing things that you need to be doing yourself," because Leon used to goof up on that job.

The last time I saw Joey was probably in 1996. He was coming into a store with two people as I was going out. There was something about him that made me do a double take, and he looked at me too. This man looked just about the way I figured Joey would look at this age. I wanted to ask him something, but he was with those other people and I couldn't think of anything to say without making him suspicious. I don't know if Joey is aware that he's Jimi Hendrix's half-brother, but there are some physical similarities through Lucille, like their cheekbones.

❧   ❧   ❧

AFTER THE DIVORCE, Lucille just indulged in whatever it was legal to do. Drugs weren't in the running like they are now, so it was just beer, wine, or any kind of alcohol. She liked that exciting, razzle-dazzle life, because she had had a taste of it when I was in the service or away. She used to quote a little ditty that she got from a movie: "Live fast, die young, and leave a good-looking corpse."

She didn't really keep in touch with the boys. I had told her she could have visiting rights, but usually she'd come around late at night, around twelve, when the boys were in bed. Sometimes she'd come by with a friend. She'd introduce me as her ex-husband, and some of the guys would feel uncomfortable. I'd say, "What the heck are you doing coming around this time of night? The kids are in bed." She'd be a little soused sometimes. She'd been drinking and just got a feeling that she wanted to come see the kids. I didn't always know where Lucille was living, because she did a lot of bouncing around. She finally lived someplace on 14th Street for a good long while. She had Pam when she was down there.

While Lucille and I were together, I could never get a car because of the way she was always goofing up with the money. Once we separated, I was finally able to get a fine old '41 Pontiac. It was a pretty sky blue with a white canvas top, and it was sharp. Jimmy, Leon, and I went up to Vancouver a lot in that old convertible to see my mother and my sister Pat and just socialize. We'd go straight up old Highway 99, the scenic route past all the homes and little farms and a long lake with a big bank along its side. The drive would take around three hours ordinarily, but if you gunned it you could make it in under two.

During one trip, my brother Frank and his wife Pearl said, "We'd like to take Jimmy and Leon off your hands for a while." Their kids, Jimmy's cousins Bobby and Diane, were also there. They were living near the house where I was born in the old Triumph Street neighborhood. It was during the summertime, so I let the boys stay up there a month or two. I went up there two or three weekends to visit them.

While Jimmy was staying in Vancouver, my mother and Pat would see him a lot. Jimmy took to wearing a green cloth vest that was part of one of my mother's stage outfits. It had little tassels on it, like a Spanish dancer's vest. He used to wear that to school. Us kids used to fool around with my mother's old costume pieces when I was young, but we would never have thought about wearing them to school, but Jimmy liked things of that sort. Of course it stood out, since it wasn't something you'd ordinarily be wearing. That vest could have been the origin of his attraction to flamboyant clothes—I'll bet that's it, because he never got into any of Lucille's things while we were living together.

Frank said that when Jimmy was staying in Vancouver with him, he got into a fight with another kid. It made Jimmy so mad he started crying. He wasn't scared of the guy, but he didn't want to hurt him. He was just really frustrated and angry. I used to do the same thing. I'd get so mad, I'd say, "They better not touch me, because I wouldn't be responsible for what I'd do to them." I never taught the boys boxing, but of course I told them, "Any kid who messes around with you, you stand up for your rights. But don't ever start a fight. Don't bully anybody." When he was a little older, Jimmy liked to tussle around with the kids out in the yard or at school, just goofing around, but he never took a regular course in wrestling or anything like that.

I was still living on Genesee in the Rainier Vista projects while Jimmy and Leon spent some of that summer in Vancouver. After they came back, things got hectic again. I was working in the daytime and there was nobody there to take care of the kids, so during the school term my sister called and told me, "Al, you got

your hands full down there. Why don't you let me take care of the boys for a while to give you a break?" I needed a little relief, so I said okay.

Pat and her husband, Joe Lashley, lived in Vancouver on Drake Street, not far from where I used to live on Richards Street. Jimmy liked his Auntie Pat and had been around her, so it wasn't a real big thing like he was going to strangers. So I took them back up there, and he and Leon got a lot of good loving care from Pat.

Pat worked as a teacher's aide, and she enrolled Jimmy in Dawson School, where I used to go as a kid. Leon was still too young to be in grade school, so he went to pre-kindergarten classes. I was paying Pat and Joe for taking care of them, and I'd run up there every Saturday to see how they were. Jimmy seemed to be doing okay, although I guess he missed me. I don't think there were any kids around there in the neighborhood where they lived, and it was mostly older people coming over to see them. Joe used to run on the railroad, so different friends of his would come by to visit.

My sister had trouble getting Jimmy to go to school while he was staying with her. She said he'd leave home early enough, but he'd gotten a lot of late charges and would sometimes miss a class or two. I asked him about it, and it turned out Jimmy was lollygagging as he was going down Granville Street, looking in store windows and just dragging his butt. I'd get after him about that. I had to spank him a couple of times in Vancouver on account of his goofing around in school.

Jimmy and Leon weren't living in Vancouver for all that long, though, because Joe Lashley died while the kids were there. Right after that Pat and the kids came down to Seattle to stay with me on Genesee. It was just a two-bedroom unit, and Pat had one room and the kids and I had the other one. She took care of the kids while I worked, and Jimmy started going to the Rainier Vista school.

Pat stayed with me until she met her second

husband, Pat Jimenez. In fact, Lucille brought him out to the house and introduced him to my sister. Pat was a Filipino. He came out there every day after they'd met, and eventually they got married. I was the best man. The preacher thought I was older than my sister, when she was about five years my senior. I said, "What?!" and Pat laughed about that. I said, "I done lived a harder life than you!"

Since my brother-in-law's first name was Pat, we used to call them "Pat and Pat." They stayed with us for a while after they got married. He'd go to Alaska to work in the canneries, and he also started landscape gardening, which he'd done before while living in Los Angeles. Pretty soon my brother Frank moved down to Seattle and started working with my brother-in-law Pat. Then Frank got a job at Boeing.

Frank and I were always close. I'd visit him and occasionally he'd come by to see me. Jimmy and Frank had a good relationship. They talked a lot. After Frank's family moved nearby, I used to go over there to get some pointers from Pearl on how to cook different things because I was the cook at home for Jimmy and Leon. I was so busy just cooking meals for those guys all the time! I'd try to fix something that would last two or three days, so we'd have meat loaf, or I'd fix up some lima beans and bacon or a big pot of spaghetti. I tried a variety of meals, but I didn't take all that much time to fix up fancy foods, because I hated to clean up. I cooked them up some good meals, but they got tired of my cooking, and Jimmy just used to say, "Dadgum, dad." But Jimmy wasn't one to be grumpy over what the food was like. He wasn't a real picky eater. He just ate it, and it didn't bother him too much.

Jimmy had an allergy to certain foods when he was small. I never once had to take him to a hospital, but I did take him to the clinic for checkups and shots, and one time I had to take him in to see the doctor for his food allergy. It turned out that orange juice or any citrus would make him break out in a rash. The doctor said this happens to a lot of kids, and Jimmy outgrew it.

As a kid, Jimmy could get out the cereal and milk, and he could make sandwiches out of bologna or peanut butter and jelly. Later on he could make scrambled eggs and bacon. He always liked bananas, apples, and watermelon, and eventually he could eat oranges. He also went for salads and hot dogs with hot Chinese mustard. Of course he'd go after cake and pie and cinnamon rolls and ice cream. He'd eat nearly anything.

❧ ❧ ❧

13 EVENTUALLY my niece Gracie, Pat's daughter, moved in with us on Genesee too, so for a while there Jimmy, Leon, and I all slept on the same double bed, while Pat and her husband Pat had the other room and Gracie slept on the davenport. Pat's husband worked until he made enough money, and then they bought a home. After they moved, Gracie said, "I gotta leave."

I said, "Can't you stay here and help until I get somebody else?"

"Oh, no. I got to leave."

"Doggone!" I said to her. "Now everybody's done gone. Who's going to take care of the kids when I'm working?" It left me high and dry, and that's when I got this girl, Edna Murray, to be our live-in housekeeper and cook.

I'd met Edna right after I got out of the army, when she happened to come by Dolores' place. She was around Lucille's age and knew her. Dolores told me that before the war Edna used to see me at dances on the weekends.

"Edna?" I said. "I just can't remember Edna." And I sure didn't notice her sitting there noticing me!

Edna was still married when I met her, and then she would come around the house to visit after Lucille and I got back together. Sometimes Lucille used to get her to baby-sit. So when I needed somebody to watch the kids, Dolores said, "Why don't you look up Edna?" So I got ahold of Edna and hired her. I paid her a salary.

Edna was a nice little gal. She was short and had fair skin and wore glasses. She was happy-go-lucky and jovial. By then she was divorced and didn't have any kids of her own, so she moved in with us. Edna was good with Jimmy and Leon. She wasn't all that mean to them, like Leon has said, but she probably didn't let them do some of the things they had no business doing. She cooked for them and made sure they made it to school. Jimmy got along with her. I'd tell him, "You mind Edna now. She's taking care of you."

Edna told me she'd had a crush on me from a long time ago. She said, "Oh, yeah, I used to watch you. Yes, I want to win you over."

"No," I said. "Let's keep this on a business level."

After getting burnt by Lucille, I was real cautious. I told Edna, "You can have your boyfriend"—because he'd come by to take her out—"and we'll just keep everything congenial."

I didn't get jealous about her boyfriend. I said, "No, I've done gone that way before." She still had her eyes on me, but I didn't want to get too wrapped up with her. Lucille came by a couple of times when Edna was there, but she didn't cause any problems. She knew Edna was taking care of the kids.

Jimmy, Leon, and I had a really good Christmas when we were still living out in Rainier Vista with Edna. Jimmy would talk about Santa Claus, and we put up a Christmas tree and all the trimmings. I got both of the kids toy trains, the wind-up kind. I got two boxes so they could make that much more track, because they'd play together. The boys were happy with the trains, and they ran them for quite a while. I told them, "Take care of your toys. When I was a kid, we'd make store-bought toys last a long time, because we didn't get them every year."

I didn't hardly have any money to be taking the kids out, but I managed to take them to the Ringling Brothers Barnum & Bailey circus. Jimmy got such a kick out of it. There were so many things to see, he said, "Doggone!" Clowns were carrying on down below, and trapeze artists were overhead. I said, "Damn! This kind of cheats you. You can't watch everything at once." Later on in his early teens Jimmy liked to go to fairs in the park. He liked thrilling rides, like a roller coaster where you'd have to be kind of a daredevil to go on it.

Edna and I lived in Rainier Vista together until I bought a home on 26th and Washington Street, and she moved in with us there. Everything was going along fine, and then my sister came around and told me that Gracie and her new husband, Buddy Hatcher, needed a place. "Yeah," I said, "but Gracie went and moved out on me on Genesee when you and your husband Pat moved. She left me high and dry, and that's when I got Edna. And now Edna's a lot of help for me."

Pat said, "But their rent is so high and they're having so much financial trouble. You should let Gracie and Buddy move in with you."

"I don't have all that much room," I told Pat. The kids had their own room, and Edna and I had the other room.

Pat finally said, "It's for the family," and so Gracie and Buddy moved in with us. Living with Gracie was tense. She did her own cooking and I did mine. Gracie was really bossy. I'd have the kids do one thing, and the next minute I'd turn around and she'd have them doing what I didn't want them to do.

Pat also talked me into letting Edna go. That was a bad move. I explained things to Edna, and she started crying. I felt like a heel. Oh, I hated that. The kids seemed to get along with Edna, and I wasn't sure how they felt about Gracie because she was ornery. ❧

JIMMY AND LEON played together pretty well. When they were hassling, it was usually something about putting their toys away. They had an equal amount of things, because I usually got the same thing for each one so there wouldn't be a squabble. So when I'd say, "Okay, you guys, time for bed—put your toys away now," Jimmy would be up and hustling things around. Leon might put an article or two away, and then he'd lay back, waiting for Jimmy to pick up some of his stuff too. I'd say, "C'mon, Leon, pick up something." He'd be moving all slow, and then I'd have to get after him. Leon was

JIMMY AND LEON, 1950.

something else.

Sometimes I'd be in the other room and I'd say, "Okay, when I come back, I want that all cleared up." And then it wouldn't be all cleared up, and they'd be putting the blame on each other. So I'd try to figure out who was hanging back and causing all the disturbance and give him a little paddy-whack.

Jimmy was a neat kid. I'd tell him, "Clean up behind yourself. Don't leave things all over, like dirty dishes. If you're going back to the kitchen, pick up your saucer and take it with you. Don't leave it there and wait for somebody else to do it." So Jimmy always cleaned up behind himself. After I made the dinner, Jimmy would do the dishes. He had other chores to do, but the main thing was for Jimmy and Leon to keep their room clean. Jimmy took good care of his clothes too—he wanted to look sharp.

Leon was more unruly than Jimmy, but Jimmy was patient with his younger brother. I'd tell him to watch Leon, and they'd go out and play together. Of course, Leon would bug him sometimes, being he was so much younger. Sometimes Jimmy wanted to play a game the right way when Leon didn't want to follow the rules.

Overall, though, Jimmy and Leon were well behaved. I got a compliment from Mrs. Harding. She and her husband had no kids, and they had a lot of old bric-a-bracs around—glass vials, little carriages and horses. Mrs. Harding had an immaculate place—I knew that because I used to clean it when I first came to Seattle. She was always telling me she wanted to see my kids, so I told her I'd come by. When Jimmy and Leon came in, she said, "Oh, their eyes got big!" because they were looking at all the little doohickies. That's like tempting a bull in a china shop, so I said, "Now you guys can

Jimmy began drawing while he was a grade schooler.

look, but don't touch a thing." And they didn't. They just sat there, and the Hardings didn't have a TV or anything for the kids to play with.

Mrs. Harding and I were in the kitchen, just talking and drinking some tea, and she said, "Maybe the kids would like some milk and cookies." So they sat there in the living room, just looking around, having their cookies and milk, and they still didn't touch a thing. She said, "Jeez, what well-behaved kids."

I said, "Oh, yeah. I told them—don't touch."

When I'd go to the store or somewhere, Jimmy and Leon would play together. I'd say, "Now, Jimmy, you watch over your little brother."

Leon just wanted to do things the opposite way, and so Jimmy would say, "Leon's always doing things he knows he's not supposed to do."

So I'd talk to Leon. "Now, you mind Jimmy, or I'm going to get on your case. Just stay out of trouble—if you can!"

Then I'd tell Jimmy, "If Leon gives you too much trouble, you just let me know."

Sometimes Jimmy would be having a hassle with Leon, and I'd hear him say, "You know what dad said." But they'd never do any fighting or duking it out around me, because Jimmy was

A GOOD SHEPHERD AND HIS FLOCK.

Jᴵᴹᴹʏ ʟɪᴋᴇᴅ sᴋᴇᴛᴄʜɪɴɢ ʜᴏʀsᴇs. I ᴛʜɪɴᴋ ʜᴇ ʟɪᴋᴇᴅ ᴛᴏ ʀɪᴅᴇ ᴛᴏᴏ.

so much bigger than Leon, and he didn't take advantage of him in that way.

Jimmy had a temper, but it took a while to get him riled up. A person would have to keep bugging him and bugging him and bugging him. He reminded me of myself, in that respect. When kids were harassing me, I'd just pass it off for a time. And then if they just kept on, I'd say, "Okay. Next time I'm going to go upside your head!" It'd be too late then.

Jimmy couldn't stand anybody who would rib somebody and then get all salty about it when the person ribbed them back. He'd say, "If you can't take it, don't try to dish it out!" I felt the same way—if you can't take a joke, don't joke

with anybody else.

Once in a while I'd catch Jimmy doing some mischievous scenes. To discipline him, I'd give him some swats on the bottom. I'd use a belt, because my hand was too heavy. I wouldn't take a heavy, big strap, but a narrow one. Jimmy would holler, "Ow, ow, ow, ow!"

I'd tell him, "That's what happens when you don't do as you're told," and that'd be it for a good while.

One time I was supposed to give him a spanking, and Jimmy said, "I'm ready, dad." I looked at him and turned my head, and I just laughed. I couldn't spank him. I just said, "You promise you won't do it again no matter what?"

But I was strict with Jimmy, and that was good for him. If a parent is too lax and lets things go, the kid loses respect for him. I've heard people say, "Oh, no, I'm not going to spank my kid. I read in a book that when they get to a certain age, they'll learn." Kids start learning right from the cradle, and if you teach them as they go along and just stay on them, you don't have to be overly strict. I've seen so many mothers with kids throwing tantrums and cussing the mothers out in public. The kids acted up because the mothers let them do the same thing at home and get away with it. Kids are going to try you. If they get away with it once, they are going to do it again and again.

A RAINBOW DRAGON.

I didn't have that trouble with Jimmy and Leon, because I never said anything more than three times. If they were wrestling around in their room at night, I'd say, "You guys be quiet and go to sleep in there." I'd say it again and tell them, "Alright, this is the last time. When I come in there, it's too late!" So they knew— three strikes and you're out!

Jimmy wasn't one of these kids who revolt. Leon would get that way sometimes, although he wouldn't do it with me so much, because Leon was a daddy's boy. He didn't know too much about his mother since he was so young when we got divorced. As time went on, though, Leon became harder to handle.

Jimmy just respected everybody. He wasn't a roustabout who'd fool around with somebody else's property. Some kids say, "Oh, let's go break some windows," or something of that sort, but Jimmy wasn't malicious in that way.

He respected everybody else's property, because I always taught him, "Don't be going around destroying other people's property. You don't like it when your property is destroyed."

Jimmy never sassed me back like some of these kids who say "No" or "Shut up." Ooh! I never said that to my folks—I just couldn't. I had to sit there and let them lecture me, and that's the way I did it with Jimmy. I'd tell him: "Be cool. Be honest with everything. Treat your fellow man as you want to be treated, just like the Good Book says. Sure, it's pretty hard sometimes, but that's the way it's supposed to be." Later on, when he got up around his teens, we could talk to each other. He'd explain things to me, and I'd hear him out. I wouldn't blow up and not give him a chance to be heard. I'd say, "Just tell me what happened —and don't lie."

I did have to get after him about fibbing. He had a way of twitching his eyes similar to the way his mother used to do it, and that would give him away. I'd say, "Hey! Don't be telling no tales." I didn't want him to become one of those habitual liars. When I was young, some of the kids I ran with would spiel off a yarn just to kill time, and then they'd get in the habit of it. All the guys knew a friend of mine was that way. They'd report something and say, "Oh, he said that." I'd say, "Aw, shoot, man. Ain't nothing to it. Forget it." He would be kidding at first, knowing that we didn't believe it. We'd be razzing him so hard, the next thing he'd get a little irritated and yell, "Yes it was!" And then he'd get to believing it himself, and he'd swear it on the bible.

Jimmy knew right from wrong. I'd be telling him about that all the time: "It's easy to start lying. You start with little bitty ones, and then it grows. So whenever people ask you questions, don't even think about saying just any old thing to get them off your back. You get used to doing that, and the next minute you'll be doing it in earnest. A lie will always catch you later on." I warned Jimmy about swearing too. When I caught him doing it, I would tell him it was wrong or give him a little spanking.

I taught Jimmy and Leon to kneel down at night to pray. To this day, I still do that by the side of my bed. I believe in the Almighty, and I believe prayer can produce change. I taught them the same prayers that my parents taught me. One of them was, "Now I lay me down to sleep, I pray the Lord my soul to keep. If I should die before I wake, I pray the Lord my soul to take." After they said that, they could do a blessing and ask for other goodies. Jimmy also knew the Lord's Prayer, and I taught him to always bless his food: "Thank you for what we are about to receive for the nourishment of our body, for Christ's sake, amen." We also had a family bible at the house.

When Lucille and I were still together, we went to a couple of churches around the neighborhood to see how they were, and after we broke up Jimmy started going to Sunday

Jimmy liked to draw futuristic cars and cartoon characters.

JIMMY'S GRADE SCHOOL CLASS PICTURE IN FRONT OF THE OLD LESCHI ELEMENTARY SCHOOL.
HE'S IN THE SECOND ROW, THIRD FROM THE LEFT, STANDING NEXT TO HIS FRIEND JAMES
WILLIAMS, WHO'S WEARING A SPORTS JACKET.

school. His grandmother would take him to the Church of God in Christ at 23rd and Madison, but I never went with Jimmy to church. I usually went to the Methodist or Baptist church, but I wasn't a regular church-goer. I didn't go for a whole lot of that show. I'd seen it as a kid, the way the preachers would blow their tops and dance and carry on behind the pulpit. It used to puzzle me, because it just seemed unnecessary.

Eventually Jimmy started going to church by himself, and he'd meet some gals there. Some of them would come by the house, wanting to go to church with him. I remember one cute little gal came by, and Jimmy went out the back door! I saw her in advance through the curtain: "It looks like somebody's here for you, Jimmy."

Jimmy said, "Tell her I'm not here! Tell her I've gone to church."

I said, "Man, that's a cute little gal. What

are you dodging her for?" I don't remember what his excuse was. Maybe he was going to run into another gal that day. He seemed to be pretty popular with the gals. Sometimes girls from school came by looking for him too, and they'd go into his bedroom. He'd always have his door open, though, and they'd be sitting there talking.

I don't know if Jimmy did any singing in church, and he was never in a choir that I know of. I don't know how Jimmy did in music at school, either, but I know he didn't have a voice. He probably couldn't sing the scales.

As he grew older, I wouldn't say Jimmy was over-religious, but he was religious in the same way that I am. I consider myself a Christian. I do all the good things and treat my fellow man the way I like to be treated. But I don't feel I have to go to church all the time to do right.

Jimmy asked me what I thought the afterlife would be like, and sometimes we'd talk about reincarnation. I think he believed in the afterlife, because sometimes he'd talk about being somewhere he'd never been before, but he'd feel like he had been there. He'd also have dreams where this same old place kept popping up.

≈ ≈ ≈

THINGS PICKED up for us when I began working for the City of Seattle, doing a regular job with the city engineers. We'd chop and saw wood, cut back brush that was hanging over sidewalks, and do various jobs of that sort. Around 1953 or '54 I bought a two-bedroom house at 2603 26th Avenue. The neighborhood was predominantly black, but there were Japanese across the street and next door. It was a nice place, but rat-infest-

ed. The rats used to get in the cupboards. The basement had been partially dug, but it was unfinished. It also had a double garage.

Jimmy liked to go out to the intersection in front of the house and play ball with the Mitchell kids, who lived across the street. Sometimes Leon would be out there too. I'd come home from work, and the kids would climb all over me. Gracie would be saying, "Get off your dad! He's tired now."

"That's okay," I'd say. "That's all right."

Then Leon and Jimmy would get to arguing. "This is my daddy."

"No! This is my daddy!"

I'd say, "Okay, you guys. I'm both you-all's dad."

Jimmy shared a bedroom with Leon on the side of the house facing the yard next door, and we just had one bed for both kids. Jimmy did a lot of drawing in grade school, and he'd put his little art projects on the dresser. They had a few posters on the wall, and Jimmy hung a flag there too.

We got our first dog after we got that house. Before then, I didn't have time for dogs because I was working so much. Then Jimmy came home one day and told me about a dog that was sitting outside the fence. Jimmy said, "Can I keep him? He followed me home. He don't have no collar or ID on him, and I'm gonna name him Prince." I looked at the dog—he was a full-grown stray—and I let him come in. I was crazy about animals—I'd been around my sister's two dogs and my niece Gracie's dog—and so I said okay.

Prince was a mixed breed, and it looked like he had some collie in him. He turned out to be a smart dog. Gracie had a little black-and-white cocker spaniel named Puddles, and they got along right

— Prince + Whitey —

off the bat. They both were
males. I had a fenced-in
yard, so the dogs mostly
stayed outside, but I let
them in the house once in
a while.

Jimmy took good care of
his dog, although I fed him
most of the time. He tried
to train him, and he took
him out for walks. Prince
was around a good long
while. Later on we got a cat
too. I was in a tavern, and
this girl came by with a box
of cats. The one I got had a
crooked tail, so we named
it Whitey Broken Tail.
Prince was used to other
animals, and he took up
with Whitey right away.
Jimmy liked to play with
the cat too. Jimmy was
good with animals—he had
that instinct.

Sometimes my sister and
I used to call Jimmy's dog
"Prince Valiant." That was
my favorite comic strip in
the newspaper, and that
was one reason why I took
that particular paper.
Jimmy and I liked to read
the same comics. Besides
"Prince Valiant," another
one we liked was "Peanuts."
Jimmy would talk about the

A BATTLE BETWEEN THE
INDIANS AND CAVALRY
— JIMMY WAS ROOTING
FOR THE INDIANS!

Here's a battle between a couple guys to see who's going to take over the throne. Kind of reminds me of "Prince Valiant," one of my favorite comic strips.

way the artist drew the little characters.

Jimmy and I used to look at comic books and eat ice cream together. He read a lot of comic books, because I'd buy them. I didn't care about Superman—he was too super-duper—but I said, "I wish they did have a man like that!" I wasn't too crazy about Batman either. But when Jimmy bought his own comics, he'd read *Batman* and *Superman*. I liked those *Amazing Stories*-type comics with the rocket ships and people zapping each other with ray guns, so Jimmy had plenty of reading material in that respect. Jimmy was fascinated by spaceships.

I used to read a lot of science fiction books and talk about saucers and such. On a good night Jimmy and I would go outside once in a while and sit out there and look at the stars. Like a lot of kids, sometimes Jimmy would look up at the sky and say, "I'd like to be up there to see what's going on on another planet." He also wondered what it was like traveling through space.

I'd say, "Ooh-wee, I wish we could see something strange." Jimmy and I would talk about how we'd like to meet an alien if some saucers floating around up there would beam us up.

One time he was having a conversation with some of his friends, and they said, "Oh, there's no other populated planet. We're the only ones."

Jimmy disagreed with them, because he'd heard me say so many times, "There's too much space up there just for one planet to be populated. With all these other galaxies, some planets have to have some inhabitants." So Jimmy always believed in that too.

Sometimes we'd look at the sky at night and think about how infinity goes on and on. I'd tell him, "Thinking about it could give you a headache. Look up at all the stars twinkling, and imagine you could just go, go, go, and you don't come to an end. It's not like you come to a wall or something. Infinity just goes on and on." Jimmy said that thinking about it gave him a headache too.

Jimmy was interested in the supernatural. We used to talk about ghosts and vampires. He used to wonder if certain things were true, such as a person coming back from the dead, or what it meant when you'd see an image of someone one second and then it'd disappear. He was fascinated by an incident that my mother said had happened to my dad. Apparently some woman had put a hex on my dad, causing him

Do-gooders trying to help the peasants. Jimmy probably got this from one of his storybooks or a movie he saw. We both liked action pictures.

to feel that a lizard was in his arm. He said he could see a fine image of the lizard right under his skin. The lizard was moving around and irritating him, so he got somebody else to break the spell.

Jimmy liked science fiction movies, naturally. He thought *The Day the Earth Stood Still* and *The Thing* were good ones. He enjoyed the old ones too, like *Frankenstein* and *Dracula*. He liked to go to the movies to see the *Flash Gordon* two-reelers, because *Flash Gordon* was all about outer space. I'd take him down to the Florence Theater, where we were able to see two regular pictures and a cartoon and newsreels for something like twenty-five cents. Sometimes his grandma Jeter would take him to the show. Jimmy would also walk or catch the bus to a theater downtown—I think it was the Capitol—because the woman who worked there got to know him, and she'd let him in for free. Jimmy liked exciting action movies, and I did too. One that we saw several times was that oldie-but-goodie *Helen of Troy*. It was a long picture, and it had a lot of action in it.

We didn't have a TV when we were living on 26th and Washington, but we did have a radio, and Jimmy and I listened to *The Shadow* and *Dick Tracy*. *Gunsmoke* was another favorite. Of course, we'd listen to anything with Jack Benny.

When the holidays came around, the teachers would have the kids make something for the parents, and Jimmy would always try to give me something. My sister would have a big spread and tell us to come down for Christmas dinner. She didn't have any kids at home, so it was just her and her husband. That all went well. I tried to give Jimmy as many things as I could. Of course, as he got older he didn't need a whole lot of toys. He started getting more clothes and things of that sort.

I remember one really good Christmas when we were living there on 26th and Washington. We had a nice Christmas tree, and I bought Jimmy one of those lightweight bikes with hand

86

brakes—that's the only bike he ever had. Jimmy was really pleased with that. He hugged me and said, "Oh, dad! Thanks, thanks, thanks!" Jimmy's cousin Bobby rode down that Christmas morning on his new bike, and they went riding. Jimmy and his cousin Bobby used to do a lot of bike riding together, and they'd decorate the bikes. Jimmy had all kinds of stuff on his. That's the way I used to do my bike too.

After we moved into our own house, Jimmy started going to Leschi Elementary School. It wasn't hard to get Jimmy to do his homework. I just left him with it on his own, because my parents didn't jump on me about my homework. I'd just notice Jimmy in the kitchen or living room doing his schoolwork, but I didn't bother him too much about it. Jimmy was just an average student.

Jimmy and his friend, James Williams, hung around together a lot. They joined the Cub Scouts, and James told me that he and Jimmy were supposed to learn how to make fires by rubbing sticks together. They went down to Seward Park, where they did start the fire. But then they got arrested or reprimanded for starting a fire in the park, and they got kicked out of the Cub Scouts because of that. Jimmy was also on the safety patrol with James Williams, directing kids at the crosswalk. He wore a little white strap across his shirt.

One time before Jimmy got a guitar, he and James Williams performed together in a talent show the school put on for parents. They were practicing around the house, working out what they were going to sing—it might have been an Ink Spots tune. They were laughing because Jimmy had taken after his mother when it came to his voice—when Lucille would try to sing, she'd hit those sour notes.

James Williams used to come by the house on Sundays, and I'd give him and Jimmy breakfast together. Jimmy called him "Potato Chips," and his nickname for Jimmy was "Henry," because of our last name. James was a little bit younger than Jimmy, and he told me that Jimmy used to stand up for him all the time. Jimmy and James Williams quit hanging around together when Jimmy went in the service. James went in the service too, but this was after Jimmy went in.

When Jimmy was around ten, he finally learned to swim. I didn't get to see him do much swimming, but I was always glad for him to learn. This older kid named Jerry would come by and take Jimmy down to Lake Washington to go swimming. He was a white kid who lived just a couple of doors up the street. The first time he told me he wanted to take Jimmy swimming, I asked him, "Can you swim good?"

He said, "Oh, yeah." He had one leg that was a little shorter than the other, but he was a good swimmer.

"Okay," I said, "now you watch him." Jimmy enjoyed it. He wanted to go back, and Jerry started taking him to the beach. It was just down the hill, less than ten minutes away.

Sometimes Jimmy stayed overnight at my

sister's place down near Lake Washington. Jimmy and James Williams also used to go there just to yackety-yack with her. Other times Jimmy would go over to his Uncle Frank's and run around with his cousin Bobby.

Jimmy liked to go freshwater fishing around Lake Washington. He had gear, but he didn't have a fishing pole. He also liked to make models of boats. He'd buy model battleships that were already painted, and he'd stick them together and put on the decals. He liked that intricate work of putting them together. I kind of liked working on them myself.

❧   ❧   ❧

JIMMY LOVED nature. He went camping one time when he was in the Cubs, and he also might have gone camping when he was staying in Vancouver with my brother. I always wanted to go camping with Jimmy, but I was so busy working I didn't have time for it.

Jimmy was also interested in going to the aquarium and museums. He especially liked to go to the museum in Vancouver to look at old Indian artifacts. He and James Williams may even have hunted for artifacts, because Jimmy became interested in some of the local Indians, like Chief Stealth and Chief Seattle—of course, he'd been dead a long time, but Seattle was named after him.

The Indians were treated really bad in those days. As a matter of fact, in some respect they got treated worse than the blacks did. Even in Seattle, they weren't allowed to go into liquor stores or taverns until the '40s or '50s. They

couldn't buy any whiskey or wine. The only way they got it was through bootleggers or friends who'd give it to them around the corner or bring it over to their house. If you got caught selling an Indian any alcohol, you'd be arrested.

Jimmy didn't like the way the Indians were treated, and of course I didn't either. Jimmy used to say, "They always make the Indians look so stupid in the movies! They're attacking the wagon train, and they ride around it making targets out of themselves. 'Hey! Knock me down. Hit me if you can!'"

I didn't like it either, and I told Jimmy, "They didn't do nothing of that sort." But that's all I ever did see when I was a kid and went to the theater. I didn't think too much of it when I was small, but as I got older it bothered me, and it bothered Jimmy too. ❧

JIMMY TRIED HIS HAND AT CARTOONS.

JIMMY ENJOYED sports, especially football. He'd also go out there and play sandlot baseball games. I had an old glove that I let him use, since he pitched right-handed. Jimmy went to one of the semi-pro games in Seattle with my brother-in-law, but I didn't pay any attention to pro baseball, because they didn't have many blacks playing on the teams.

Jimmy fooled around with sandlot basketball at the

school grounds, and he played touch football out there with the kids. Naturally as he got more into it he became interested in the pro teams. He'd get to talking with some of his friends about the different teams, and he drew a lot of pictures of the different teams and their emblems.

He liked the underdog. Sometimes he'd be pulling for a team that was behind, hoping they'd pick up and start getting the upper hand. He felt sorry when one side was getting clobbered, but he'd laugh about it at the same time. "Man, them guys sure got clobbered!" he'd say. "I sure feel sorry for them getting beat so bad."

Jimmy played for the Fighting Irish, a Little League football team, for two years in a row, and he liked it. One of the kids who played on Jimmy's team told me that only one member of the Fighting Irish was actually Irish. When Jimmy would go out to practice with the team, I'd say, "Yeah, I wish they had something like that when I was a kid." Jimmy was serious about it, although he never was all that muscular. He was just average size, and I don't recall ever seeing him working out doing push-ups or any of that.

The Fighting Irish played

J IMMY DREW THESE WHEN HE PLAYED FOOTBALL. HE DIDN'T COLLECT FOOTBALL CARDS, SO HE MUST HAVE SEEN THE TEAMS ON TV OR READ ABOUT THEM IN THE NEWSPAPER.

at different places, and I went to all the games. They'd try to let all the kids participate in every game, and the coaches would say that the parents were more trouble than the kids. A lot of the parents would say, "Aren't you going to let my kid play more?" Jimmy was a lineman. He might have got bopped around a little bit, but he never got hurt seriously enough to go to the hospital.

Jimmy did most of his drawing when he was going to school and playing football. My brother Leon and I also did a lot of drawing when we were kids, so it ran in the family. Like Jimmy, I drew a lot of battles. Every page of my history book would have a nice landscape with airplanes or soldiers running back and forth. Jimmy especially liked drawing and sketching. He'd sit down at a table and get out some crayons or an ordinary pencil and draw some imaginary or real objects. He never had art classes that I knew of, but he might have taken it in school. He had a good hand and his own ideas and imagination, and at one time he thought about being a commercial artist.

Jimmy drew a lot of outer space pictures of strange planets and spacemen. He also drew quite a few football action scenes and

pictures of speedboat races and fancy cars. Around this time he became interested in midget cars and saw some car races. After he formed the Experience, he still liked races. I have a photo that he took of a big pileup at one of the Indianapolis races. He did a lot of talking about it, and evidently he'd taken a picture of the TV screen while they were showing it.

We always had decks of cards around the house, and Jimmy and Leon liked to play Old Maid and Casino and War—all them kid games. Jimmy also played tonk—a lot of grown-ups played that. I liked to play cards myself, especially lowball and stud poker, but I didn't play around the house. I'd do it elsewhere. Jimmy didn't play poker that I know of, and he didn't seem to be too much into gambling unless he'd make a two-bit football bet with one of his friends: "Oh, I'll bet you that so-and-so is going to win."

To My DAD FROM YOUR SON ON YOUR BIRTHDAY!

❧ ❧ ❧

WHILE WE WERE still living on 26th Avenue, I lost the job with the city and was unemployed again. Then I went to work in the shipping department at Bethlehem Steel. We wrapped hot-metal support rods with wire after they came down off of big rollers. Then we'd clean around the place, take hammers and knock chips off the steel, and do all kinds of other work around the mill. It was the dirtiest job I ever had. I never did wash any clothes. We'd just throw them away because they were so torn up. We'd

JIMMY DREW HIS SHARE OF BATTLE SCENES.

95

put on two or three pairs of pants at a time because they'd get so dirty. I never knew how much money I was getting paid because each check was different. I didn't work there very long, though, and pretty soon I was out of work again.

To make a little money, I started to collect scrap metal—copper wire, brass, aluminum. I had learned about that when I was a kid, hustling to make money, and here I was still doing it. I'd burn the insulation off the copper wire and take a stick and knock the ashes off. Then I'd put the copper wire in a box and take it to the recycling place.

Jimmy came up a hard way. We weren't rich by a long shot, and most times we would be

He'd say, "Oh, I understand."

Jimmy's shoes had holes in them and his clothes were out of fashion, but they were clean. I cut Jimmy's hair, and he'd say, "Oh, daddy, you're cutting it too close," or something like that. I wasn't a barber, but I had a hair-cutting set, and I kept his hair cut pretty good. Then when he started noticing girls—or they started noticing him—we'd go to the barbershop.

A lot of times we had to eat horsemeat. I never did eat any steak, although I often thought about it. There were places in the Pike Place Market with big signs advertising horsemeat. It was cheaper, and when you cooked it, ground horsemeat didn't shrivel up as much as regular hamburger. It tasted okay to me. It didn't seem to bother Jimmy, because I told him what it was. He would eat it like me, and he wouldn't be finicky.

I told a girl that I was going with at that time, "I'll fix you up a burger."

"Oh, that sounds good."

We were chomping away and she was licking her chops, and she said, "Ooh, this is good."

"Haven't you ever eaten any horsemeat?"

She said, "No! And I don't want to!"

I was going to tell her it was horsemeat after she was through eating, but on second thought I said to myself, "No, I don't think so."

Then she asked me, "Why'd you bring that up?"

"I was just thinking about getting some sometime. I was just wondering."

"No way," she said. "I would know it if I ate it."

I went hungry sometimes to feed the kids. Before I ate, I made sure that there was always something left over so Jimmy and Leon could have a second helping. I used to tell Jimmy, "Don't ever waste food, because it will come

below average. But Jimmy wasn't one to be crying the blues all the time if he didn't have this or that. He just went along with it. Jimmy knew how hard I struggled and worked to make a life for him. I used to tell him, "Everybody has hard times. We're scuffling right now and hardly got anything to eat, but it ain't going to be like this all the time."

back on you. There's too many hungry people in the world, and I've been hungry." Jimmy had a good constitution. He had to, with the rough time we had there.

Two or three different times we didn't pay the light bill, and so the lights were turned off and we used candles. We kept warm with an oil-circulated heater, and we'd take off the lid to make toast on top.

I was right in that age bracket where people thought I was too old for different kinds of work. I'd try to get a job, because I'd taken electrical TV training under the GI Bill and was qualified. I went down to get a job at Poole Electric as a TV helper, and this guy said, "You got the know-how, but your age is a problem because you'd have to do some pole climbing."

I said, "There ain't nothing to that. To me it isn't a problem." But I was close to forty, and they wanted younger people—or so they told me.

I don't know if they called it Jim Crow where I was living, but I know that if you were black you couldn't get a lot of jobs that you ordinarily could get now. You'd see a job advertised in the paper, go down and apply, and they'd say, "It's just been taken." Two or three days later it'd still be in the paper. Or you'd call there and they'd tell you to come in. Then after they saw you, they'd say, "Somebody just beat you to it," and all that kind of stuff. Sometimes you'd know it was a race issue.

I didn't have to teach Jimmy about the inequality faced by black people in America. It just came along. You grew up that way. But I did tell him, "In the North, you got more privileges. Down South you don't have many at all. In some places down South you have to get off the sidewalk for a white person. But up here we're still discriminated against when it comes to getting good jobs." Of course Jimmy and I were aware

JIMMY'S DRAWING OF A "C-C-RAZY" CONCERT.

of the demonstrations and race riots during the civil rights days, and we understood what was going on down South. People got tired and said, "It's finally just got to come to a head."

   ❧   ❧   ❧

EVENTUALLY Gracie wanted to move from our house on 26th, and everything got all screwed up. It left me holding the bag again. That was some old hectic times. I couldn't make the payments, so everything was just going down the drink.

Leon, who was becoming more unruly, began staying with Pat and her husband down near the lake. Then Pearl and Frank convinced me it was better for Jimmy to stay with them, so it would be easier for me to get around. So Jimmy went to stay in their house on John Street near Meany Junior High School. He shared a room upstairs with Bobby. He took his bike with him, because he and Bobby rode around together. I'd go by and visit and see how it was going. Sometimes Jimmy would be out playing with Bobby, or they'd come by the house to see what I was doing.

Jimmy thought a good deal of Pearl and Frank. They had a record player, and Bobby remembers that that's when Jimmy became really interested in music. Jimmy liked to listen to a 45 of Elvis Presley's "You Ain't Nothing But a Hound Dog," and he liked Little Richard's 45s. When he was around fourteen, Jimmy went to an Elvis concert to see what it was all about. I didn't go with him. In fact, I didn't know too much about Elvis myself until after Jimmy was in the service. But Jimmy liked

Elvis, and he sketched a picture or two of him. I've heard Jimmy and Elvis met at an airport after Jimmy began performing as the Experience. There's supposed to be a photo of them shaking hands, and I'd sure like to see that.

While Jimmy was staying with Frank and Pearl, Cornell and Ernestine moved in with me. We always called them "Ben and Ernie." Ben's real name was Cornell Benson. I first met him at Ray's Pool Hall on Jackson Street near 24th, just after the Korean War. Benson had been drafted, and he still wore a uniform. I'd stop by the hall, and we'd shoot pool together. Ben was a good shooter, and I was pretty good myself. We were there a good deal of the time, especially on the weekend. Ernestine lived down the street. I don't know how she and Ben met, but she'd walk up around our way, going to the store or something, and he'd stand out there and be whistling at her. They got to talking, and it was one of those things. Ernie was a good-looking little gal.

Ben and Ernie stayed at the house less than a year, and then later on Jimmy and I lived with them for a while. Jimmy got along fine with

JIMMY WITH MY BROTHER FRANK AND HIS WIFE. JIMMY'S COUSIN BOBBY IS IN THE WHITE SHIRT, AND THE LITTLE GIRL IS BOBBY'S SISTER DIANE. THEY WERE VISITING FRIENDS IN WALLA WALLA WHEN THIS WAS TAKEN AROUND 1958.

JIMMY WAS INSPIRED BY ELVIS.

"Honey Don't"
"Hound Dog"
"love me Tender"
"i need your lovin"
"Too Much"
"Playing for keeps"
"Blue Suede Shoes"
"Don't be Cruel"
"My Baby left me"
"Rip it up"
Paritized
"i want you i need you i love you"
Parilized
Heart breack
"Don't be Cruel"
"love me tender"
"Too Much"
"Hound Dog"
"Blue Suede Shoes"
"Love me Tender"
"My baby left me"
"Peace in the Vally"
"Don't be Cruel"

I TOOK JIMMY AND LEON TO THE CIRCUS WHEN THEY WERE YOUNG.

and Mrs. McKay made the meals. She lived there with her husband, and there was an elderly guy who was a roomer there too. Jimmy wasn't with me when I moved to Mrs. McKay's, but soon after that he came over to stay with me, and the two of us were together again. Jimmy and I had the front room upstairs, and we shared a bed. We could also use certain areas of the house, like the kitchen, bathroom, and front room. This was around 1956, and we spent about a year there. We had one Christmas at Mrs. McKay's, but we didn't have a tree that time.

Ben and Ernie. They were nice people and real close buddies. Ernie and I joked and laughed all the time. She'd laugh at me laughing. Naturally when I'd get to laughing real hard, tears would come out of my eyes and it would look like I was crying. I'd be wiping my eyes, and she'd look at me and start cracking up. Her maiden name was Tobey, and she'd come from a pretty large family. I'd say, "All you Tobeys got that harshy laugh. You're the terrible Tobeys!" We had a riotous time.

They called me "Bodacious" because I used that expression a lot. I'd say, "Don't be so bodacious, you clobber-headed idjit!" I got that from Snuffy Smith in the comics. They also called me "dad." They were younger than me, but they weren't all that much younger for me to be their dad. But I'd sit there and give them fatherly speeches when they'd be quarreling over one thing or another. They finally got married, and then they really did fight after that!

When I wasn't able to make the payments any longer, I lost the house and moved into a room at Mrs. McKay's boardinghouse on 29th Avenue. It was a room-and-board situation,

Jimmy would still go over to play at Frank and Pearl's house. After a while they moved from John Street to Yesler Way, right across from the Leschi Elementary School. Shortly after that, though, Frank and Pearl got divorced. I don't know what happened between them, because I never asked. It was none of my business. Pearl always had the kids with her after that, and Frank paid child support. Pearl, Bobby, and Diane lived in Seattle for a while, and then they moved to Spokane. Pearl and my mom stayed friends all the way down the line, and eventually they lived together in Vancouver.

❧   ❧   ❧

JIMMY WASN'T around Leon much after Leon was about seven. Of course Leon says, "Oh, yeah, he was around me," but Jimmy wasn't. While Leon was staying with Pat down

JIMMY DID A LOT OF RIDING WITH HIS COUSIN BOBBY.

near Lake Washington, he became unmanageable, and finally Pat said she just couldn't handle it. That's when I contacted the child welfare people. A caseworker told me, "Jimmy's older and there's not so much pressure on him, but it's better to let Leon go. He's smaller and needs to be in a foster home."

I said, "Okay, I understand that, especially with me being out of work." So that's what happened. Jimmy stayed with me all the time, while Leon went to foster homes. Jimmy took it pretty hard,

although they didn't do all that much running around together anyway, since there was a five-year difference in their ages. Leon stayed for a while with some people I knew very well, the

Wheelers. They had two kids of their own, and they took care of two or three others besides Leon. They didn't live very far from Jimmy and me. Leon went from there to other people that I also knew.

Sometimes Jimmy would go by and visit his brother, but he was with a different crowd than Leon. By then Jimmy was hanging around with Sam Johnson, and I know Sam didn't want to be hanging around where Leon was. The last place Leon stayed, though, was just up the street, and so he started coming down to see us once in a while on the weekend. Then when he was fifteen or sixteen, Leon started staying permanently with me again. But Jimmy was in the service by then, so he was gone from home.

There are a few other things Leon has said that I'd like to clear up. Some books mention how Jimmy met Little Richard while we

Jimmy drew all kinds of crashes.

were living on Yesler Way, but Jimmy wasn't there—nobody was there for that! That was a tale that started when a reporter interviewed Leon. When I read about it in the newspaper, I said, "Oh, man, what the hell is this? Ain't that something—Leon said that Little Richard had come by our house in a limousine!" I had heard of Little Richard back then, but Little Richard didn't know us from Joe Blow. I just flipped when I saw that.

I told Leon, "Now where in the hell, Leon, did you get that?"

He said, "Oh, yeah! Little Richard came by."

"Where was I? How come I didn't see Little Richard?"

"You weren't home at the time."

"What the hell was Little Richard doing over there when we didn't even know Little Richard? Why would Little Richard be coming by to talk to us?"

At the time Little Richard supposedly came by, Leon was staying at the foster home right up the street from us. He said

INTERCEPTED

that the church his foster parents went to was the same one Little Richard's mother or grandmother went to. I said, "Yeah, but Little Richard's folks don't live here. They live elsewhere."

"Well, he stopped by there."

I said, "Leon, that's a damn lie. You know it is. Little Richard didn't know Jimmy. Now why would he be coming by to see him? Jimmy wasn't even playing the guitar then. Jeez!" On top of that, the people at the confectionery store across the street, the Wilsons, saw everything that went on. And they would have been asking me, "Ooh, whose limousine was over there, Al?" So I know nothing like that happened. I don't know if that story was one of Leon's fantasies or where he got that from. Maybe he just felt like he had to say something to the news. He also says that I used to leave him and Jimmy sitting out in the car half the night while I'd be shooting pool. That's not true. Once in a while I'd take Leon and Jimmy down to the Casino, a pool hall on Second Avenue. They had a Filipino restaurant there, and sometimes I'd take the kids to the restaurant, since we liked the food. Other times they'd have to wait out in the car while I'd run into the place and get some betting tabs for sports events. I'd just go in there, pull off however many tabs I felt lucky about, pay for them, put them in my pocket, and come right back out. I didn't linger around in there—there was no reason to. But Leon will swear up and down, "Yeah, dad used to take us down there and shoot pool and leave us out in the car all night."

"Man, Leon," I told him, "I ain't never did anything like that. You wouldn't be sitting there all night! As a matter of fact, you wouldn't be sitting there more than five minutes."

Leon has told another story about how one time Lucille was running away from me and tried to take off with him and Jimmy in my car. That's not true either—she didn't do that. I didn't get a car until after we split up. She was in my car one time after that, but Lucille couldn't drive, so I didn't let her get behind the wheel. She didn't have a driver's license, so I did all the driving. I don't know where Leon got these stories from. ❧

JIMMY AND I were living at Mrs. McKay's boarding-house when Lucille passed away. Even when we had our own house, Jimmy didn't have a whole lot of contact with his mother. She wouldn't call up and say she was coming by. She would just sporadically stop by. Maybe two or three weeks would go by and then all of a sudden she'd just pop in any old time.

FEB. 7, 1458   DADDY SLEEPING 1st POSE

I'd let her talk to Jimmy. He'd say, "Where you been at?"

Lucille would say, "Oh, I'm at So-and-so's." She'd be telling him about herself, and she'd talk about things she was going to bring him.

After she'd leave, Jimmy would say to me, "Dad, why does mama always do that? Mama says she's gonna get me this and she's gonna bring me that, and when she shows up, she don't have it."

"Well, your mom's forgetful. She probably forgot or doesn't have the money to buy it." I'd make all kinds of excuses for her and tell him that she meant well. He knew what the situation was, but he'd say, "I wish she wouldn't do that."

Lucille didn't come by at all after we moved to Mrs. McKay's, so I didn't see her unless I ran into her on the street, and when I did, she looked run down.

When we were on the verge of breaking up, I'd tell her, "Yeah, you're just going to work yourself to an early grave. You're going to destroy your body." But she wouldn't get all that drunk around me when we were together. That came afterwards. After I left her, then she'd be calling up soused and saying, "Come and get me."

I'd say, "You had no business being out there in the first place."

She'd say, "I wanna come home," and that kind of stuff.

She drank a lot after our divorce, and finally she ran herself into the ground. People would tell me, "Al, Lucille's just going down the tubes." Well, she was looking for *me* to go down the tubes with her and end up on skid row drinking my sorrows out of a bottle. I said, "Heck, no! I got these kids to think about. Somebody's got to take care of them."

It wound up the opposite way. Lucille ended

JIMMY MADE THIS SKETCH JUST A WEEK AFTER HIS MOTHER DIED.

up on the skids, while I was still okay. Finally she dissipated herself to where the first thing she'd do when she woke up was get a bottle of wine, a beer, or some liquor. She had a bad case of yellow jaundice at one time. She was in the hospital two or three times just before she died.

Some people who were giving me a report on Lucille said they wanted me to bring the kids to the hospital to see her because they didn't expect her to live much longer. I took Jimmy and Leon up there, but they wouldn't let us go past a certain floor because the kids were underage. I said, "But their mother's deathly sick, and it's her request that she wants to see the kids before she dies." But no, the hospital staff wouldn't let me take Jimmy and Leon up there. Lucille survived that time. There was another time they didn't think she was going to live, but Lucille pulled through again. I went there to see her, and she said, "Oh, yeah, I know what you gonna say to me."

The last time I saw Lucille, it looked like she'd aged a lot. About a month before she died, she had gotten married again, and I met her husband. His name was Al Mitchell, and he was a retired stevedore. He was older than I was.

Lucille passed away on February 2, 1958. Al Longacre, who used to go with her, told me about it. He came over and said, "I got some sad news, Al. Lucille died last night."

I said, "Oh, well, it's not surprising." My understanding is that she had some kind of a hemorrhage.

I told Jimmy about it. Oh, he felt sorrow over his mother's death, and he cried. I know her death affected him deeply, but I don't know what went on in his mind. He might have been a little mad at his mother for living the kind of life she lived. Lucille just cut her life short.

Jimmy wanted to go to her funeral, but at the time I didn't have a car to take him in, and I didn't want to go. So I gave him carfare and told him, "Well, you got the fare, so you can catch the bus," but he didn't go. My mother came down for the funeral. I'd thought about going, but I just wanted to remember Lucille the way I last saw her.

I ran into Ernestine a few days later, and she was laughing. "Oh, yeah," she said. "I saw your ex just the other day, and she was staggering down the street."

I said, "Yeah. Well, she won't be staggering anymore. She just died."

Ernie said, "Oh, I'm so sorry." She didn't know Lucille was gone, and she felt so bad about that.

JAMES HENDRIX PER. II ROW 2.   "57"

Later on Jimmy and I would talk about Lucille. Although he probably remembered fun times with her, he never mentioned them a lot. Sometimes he'd say, "Yeah, I had a good-looking mama," and things like that. One time he said to me, "I wonder why mom just didn't take care of herself better." Another time he mentioned, "I wish mom hadn't been the way she was, carrying on and all that."

Jimmy loved his mother, but he knew how she was. She loved him, but in her own strange way. She talked about, "Oh, yeah, I have so many kids," but she didn't take care of any of them all the way down, and she didn't have any with her when she died.

Leon didn't know Lucille that well, and he told me that now he doesn't remember her. Joey, of course, didn't know anything about her. Jimmy was the only one who remembered his mother. Lucille was thirty-two when she passed away. Jimmy might have been learning guitar by then, but his mother never heard him play. I feel so sad about that.

❧   ❧   ❧

JIMMY STARTED writing poems and ditties before he got into playing music. Then one day when we were at Mrs. McKay's boardinghouse, I went down to the store after I'd told him to sweep up the room. When I came back he'd cleaned up, but at the foot of the bed was a little pile of broken straws. I said, "Hey, I thought you were supposed to clean up. What are all these straws doing at the foot of the bed?"

Jimmy said, "Oh, I did clean, and then I was sitting there making believe the broom was a guitar." He was strumming the broom, and that's where the pile of straws came from.

The landlady had a son who was a grown man. His name was James too. He had an acoustic guitar, and he'd sit out on the porch and play blues and different numbers. Jimmy and I would sit out there and listen. A lot of times when I wasn't there, Jimmy would be sitting there listening to him. One day Jimmy said to me, "James wants to sell the guitar to me for five dollars, and I'd like to get it."

I said, "Okay." I gave him the five dollars, and that was the first guitar he ever had. It was a right-handed guitar, and at first Jimmy started playing right-handed. Then I saw him changing the strings and playing left-handed. I

said, "How come you're playing left-handed?"

"I find I can play left-handed easier than I can right-handed."

"Well, do your own thing." I didn't even question it. I just let it go on.

It didn't bother Jimmy to have me or anybody else around while he was trying to learn, because he'd be concentrating so hard on his playing. He'd get into it, just like a person plunking away with one finger on a piano. One of the first things that he learned how to play was the theme song from *Peter Gunn*, so even when he was just starting, he would make music out of the guitar. Who knows—playing guitar could have been his way of working through some of his feelings about his mother.

❧   ❧   ❧

FROM MRS. McKAY'S, Jimmy and I moved in with Gracie and Buddy in their home at 1434 Pike Street at 29th. They had a rec room downstairs, and that's where Jimmy and I had our quarters. We had our own entrance in the front of the house, and we shared the same bed. The house hasn't changed much since we lived there. Gracie still had her dog Puddles, and we had Whitey and Prince. We lived there not quite two years, and Whitey died while we were staying there.

I paid rent, naturally. Gracie was still a little fussbudgety, but we got along okay. Buddy was a regular guy. They had children—Patty, Leona, and Diane. Gracie would get on Jimmy's nerves, and her kid Patty was a pain when she was growing up. Patty would just do things to irritate you, and then double-dog dare you to say anything about it. She would stand right in front of the TV, for instance, while we were watching a show. Someone would say, "Patty, move."

"But I'm watching TV."

"Well, we are too, and you're standing between us and the TV!" She would also get real whiny and stubborn.

When people bothered him, Jimmy would just go out and get out of sight and sit somewhere and think. He was out with his friends a good deal of the time too.

Jimmy was going to Garfield High School by then and hanging around with Sam Johnson and a kid named Leo—I forget his last name. Jimmy also hung around with Sam after we moved to East Terrace, so he knew him for a long time. Sam was a tall, slim, nice-looking kid who played the bass. He probably showed Jimmy how to play a few things, and some of Jimmy's other friends showed him a few chords. Jimmy would pick up a little bit here and there, and he learned a lot of stuff on his own. I never did get him a guitar book or lessons.

He liked to play his guitar out in the yard. Sometimes a kid up the street would come down and they'd play music out in the back yard together. He played guitar behind James Williams too, because James wanted to be a crooner.

Not long after Jimmy started playing guitar, we went down to Seattle's annual Seafair boat race at Lake Washington. We were at my sister's place, where they had a big spread out on the lawn. You could easily walk from their place down to the pits for the boat races. It was all family, and Jimmy was there with Sam Johnson. Sam had his bass and Jimmy had his guitar. They had been rehearsing some music

to play for us, and so they set up and said, "Okay. A little entertainment."

They'd get to playing, and being beginners, one of them would hit a bad note or get a little mixed up. They'd just stop and tell us, "Wait a minute! Wait a minute!" Then they'd go back over it again and make another goof-up and say, "Wait a minute! Wait a minute!" That kept going on, so I said, "Okay, you guys, give us our money back!" I was just teasing them, and we all laughed.

Seafair runs for two weeks every year. It's something like Mardi Gras, a big celebration for all of Seattle. They have parades in all the different districts and a big grand finale torchlight parade with floats and fireworks. During the last day— usually a Sunday—they have the hydroplane races on Lake Washington.

A long time ago people would gather halfway across the floating bridge, where they'd get a good view of the boats. One of the famous drivers, Bill Munsey, used to roar out from right underneath the bridge. Jimmy and a friend were standing out there on the floating bridge one time when a boat did a flip in the air and the driver got killed. Jimmy came back and said, "Oh, dad, I saw that accident." He explained to me how the boat lifted up in the air, and he made drawings of a scene like that.

While we were living at Gracie's, Jimmy had an afternoon paper route delivering the *Post Intelligencer*. He didn't have his bike any more, so

he'd just sling the paper bag on his shoulder and carry the papers around. He had so much trouble collecting money from people, though, he didn't have the route very long. I knew how that was, people always telling the kid to come back next week. I even had to pay the newspaper company some money because of some of the people not paying Jimmy. It was a hassle.

Jimmy liked being in the outdoors, especially in the winter, when we'd go sledding. Gracie's place had a nice steep hill right in front, and when it snowed a lot of cars couldn't traverse up that hill. Jimmy and I would get out there with the sled. I'd sit down first and he'd get on back, and we'd sled down two blocks of hills and coast all the way to what's now called Martin Luther King Way.

JIMMY LEFT home one time while we were staying with Gracie and Buddy, but I didn't even know he was gone. He used to go over to this boy Pernell Alexander's place. Pernell was older than Jimmy and James Williams, and he was being raised by his grandmother. Jimmy and James looked up to Pernell like a big brother.

The one time Jimmy ran away—well, I don't know if Jimmy himself would call it "running away"—he was over there at Pernell's grandmother's. Before that, though, he used to ask me if he could spend the night there. Pernell's grandmother was all right—there was nothing wrong with her. Sometimes I was leery of Pernell, though, because he was so much older and fast-talking. I told Jimmy, "Now, you

JIMMY WAS CRAZY ABOUT
CAR RACES.

watch out for Pernell. Don't let him be teaching you anything that you're not supposed to be doing." I knew that Jimmy was easygoing, and he trusted people.

Then one day Buddy Hatcher came by and asked me if Jimmy had showed up.

I said, "What do you mean, has Jimmy showed up? What's going on?"

"Didn't he run away?"

"Not that I know of." So if he was running away, I had a good idea where he was, so maybe it was a halfway runaway. Even our dog Prince used to go over to Pernell's and come back.

When I found Jimmy, all I told him was, "You should let me know where you're at." He never ran away on any other occasion.

After they got married, Benson and Ernestine were living at 1715 College Street. From Gracie's, Jimmy and I moved in with Ben and Ernie, but we weren't there for too terribly long. Benson and Ernestine had their living quarters, and Jimmy and I had one room. I paid rent, although I didn't charge them any when they were with me. Ernestine's sister and her husband lived in another house nearby.

While we were there I bought a little Ford pickup truck, a real rattletrap, for a hundred dollars. The motor was really good, but that was the only good thing about it. The body was shot. I think it was a '36, and I kept it on the parking strip down below the house.

Jimmy and I enjoyed sitting around playing Monopoly at Benson's. I was always buying up the skid row places. We all got into it, and we'd play late into the night on a weekend to see who was going to get all that money. It was a lot of fun.

Jimmy started going out with Betty Jean Morgan, his teenage sweetheart. She was his first girlfriend, and they were pretty tight. He brought her by the house a couple of times with her little brother. She seemed fair to me from what I knew about her, but I didn't know her right down to the T. She was courteous and nice. Whenever they'd go into his bedroom, they'd always leave the door open.

Jimmy had run around with some little girls before that, walking them to church or coming from school, but he wasn't serious about any one particular girl before Betty Jean. I told Jimmy, "When you're going out with girl-friends, you've got to watch yourself. I hope you don't go around getting any girls pregnant when you can't even take care of yourself."

After my brother Frank got remarried to Mary, Jimmy and I would go by their duplex on 27th Avenue a lot. Frank and Mary both worked at Boeing, and she had no kids. Mary was real nice, and Jimmy liked her. We were friendly with their neighbors too, so we'd run back and forth visiting everybody. Sometimes we'd all get together and play cards or one of them would have a party. While he was married to Pearl, Frank was a homebody. Then after he got married to Mary, he was a little more outgoing and not so much of a family man. They'd go to a lot of dances and social affairs.

I finally started making money by working with my brother-in-law Pat. He had his own

NOV 29, 1957   ORANGE BLACK   MAROON + GOLD
SAN JOSE SPARTANS ARIZONA STC.

landscaping business, and he seemed to be doing pretty good at it. At first I'd do odd jobs for him on the weekends, and then I started working pretty regular with him. He liked to go to Alaska during the canning season early in the spring, so I'd take care of the business while he was gone. Then he'd come back in the summer and resume, and I'd still work for him. I handled his truck and all the workers on the truck.

When I first started out, I was doing a lot of stuff the way Pat was doing it. As I became more adept, I found easier ways to do the job while putting out the same production. I'd show my brother-in-law shortcuts, and here he'd been doing it a whole lot longer than me.

But he wouldn't buy the equipment that we needed; he wanted to play it too cheap. I said, "Dadgum, Pat. Why don't you get some of these other tools? They make gardening easier, and they got 'em for sale."

"But they cost too much."

"Yeah, but it's a business write-off for your income tax, and it makes the job easier and faster."

When I first started with Pat, we'd go along the edge of the lawn with little hand clippers. Then they came out with long-handled clippers that let you go around the edge without squatting down, so you could go a whole lot faster. Pat hated to put money out, though, so

I bought a pair of my own. Pat said, "Ooh, I gotta get some."

"Yeah," I said, "you ought to get some for the other guys—these are mine!" Pat just skimped too much.

I got paid by the hour, and when I saw how much money I was making for Pat, I said, "Hell, I think I'll go into business for myself." I did landscaping from then on until the late '70s.

I always liked the outdoors, and I was happier doing gardening than any of my other jobs. I was my own boss, and I could name my own price. It was up to me to make the money, and that's the reason why I liked it. I usually charged a flat fee for the summer. I was conscientious about my work, and I wanted to satisfy the people.

Jimmy and I had to move from Ben and Ernie's place after the owner came over to inspect the house. He noticed the room Jimmy and I had and asked them if somebody was living there. They told him about us, and the owner said that Jimmy and I had to move.

With me working again, we were able to move to 1314 East Terrace, where we had an apartment on the second floor. We had two rooms, a kitchen, and a bedroom. This was somewhere around 1959, and those were raggedy old apartments. I never even had

the gas stove turned on because there were so many cockroaches running around the place. I didn't see any mice around because the millions of roaches outdid the mice! And when you've got them all through the building, there's no use in trying to kill them in your section. We'd go in a room and hear the rustle of all the cockroaches running out of the light. Jimmy and I just learned to live with it.

There was very little of anything right about that ramshackle old apartment. There wasn't any use in complaining, though. We just said, "Well, we'll have to live here. This is the best we can do right now."

While our apartment was quiet, it was rowdy down on Terrace Street. A couple of doors from us people were sitting out on the porch in the summertime, drinking beer and making noise and hollering. Folks were prostituting themselves on the street and around the block. There were a couple of houses of prostitution right across the street. Jimmy knew what was going on. That was a rough neighborhood, and they finally closed that street off altogether and tore those apartments down.

Prince, who was getting old, disappeared while we were living there. The apartment house had a door downstairs, and Prince would scratch for me to let him out. He'd go do his business and come back in. We had a front window, so I could look out to see where he was. Then he injured his leg in an accident or fight. We took him to the vet, and after he came back, he wanted to go outside. He was gone for a good long while, so I checked with the pound. He was there, so I got him out.

Not long after that I let Prince out one evening, and he didn't come back. I wasn't too worried at first, since Prince used to go over to Benson's place, and every once in a while Ernestine's sister would call me up and say, "Al, Prince is over here visiting. He's sitting on the porch."

I'd say, "He'll come on home," and sure

enough he would.

He knew where all the family lived, because he used to go by my brother's place too. My sister-in-law Mary would say, "Yeah, Prince is just like a little old man, going around visiting the family." He'd sit up on their porch for a while too.

But we never did see Prince again after I let him out that night. Jimmy was upset. We walked all around the neighborhood looking for him and checked with the pound, but we never saw him again.

❧   ❧   ❧

NOT LONG AFTER we moved to East Terrace, I got Jimmy his first electric guitar at Meyers Music. I also asked them if they had any cheap saxophones, because I wanted to get one for me. They had an old C-melody sax, the kind used in a marching band. I didn't know the difference and wasn't going to get anything real fancy anyway, so I got that sax at the same time I got Jimmy's electric guitar.

I'd never played sax before that, but I always liked the instrument. I liked the piano too, but I said, "The piano costs too much and it's a little too big to carry around." We never had a piano around, but I did see Jimmy plunk on the piano when we'd go somewhere where somebody had one. A sax was just a lot easier to transport. Eddie Harris was one of my favorite sax players at that time, and Coleman Hawkins too—he was from way back when I was jitter-bugging. But after I got the sax and got Jimmy the guitar, I was more interested in the guitar.

Since people on Terrace were always sitting out drinking beer on their porches, it didn't make any difference about the noise we made, so I'd blow the sax and Jimmy'd be plunking on the guitar. I didn't know anything about a sax, so I was just tootin' around trying to find the

scale. Jimmy would tease me that I was playing the same way you'd see a person trying to play piano with one finger—*ding, ding*. That's the way we both would do it. We were blasting, though Jimmy didn't have an amplifier. I never did get him an amplifier, although I'd planned on it. But he got music out of his guitar as it was. When he went over to some of his friends' places, he'd use their amps. He didn't complain about it.

I got behind in the payments on the instruments, and the lady from the store said, "One of them has to go back."

I said, "Well, I'll let the sax go back because Jimmy's going to do more with the guitar than I am with the sax. I just got it for enjoyment."

Jimmy never took music lessons, but once he got that electric guitar, every day he would be plunking on it. Jimmy tried playing lead guitar right away, because the guitar I got him was a regular six-string lead guitar. Jimmy always said, "Oh, boy, if I could get to doing like So-and-so on the guitar," and he just worked at it and worked at it, practicing day and night. He played the guitar *every* day. He carried it around with him at all times, although I don't believe Jimmy ever took his guitar to high school, like some people have claimed, unless they had some special class or event where he needed it.

After school Jimmy would go down to a community club on 18th Avenue. This was a place for teenagers, something like the YMCA. They had pool tables, although I don't know how much pool Jimmy used to shoot. If he wasn't there, he'd be hanging around with some of his friends, playing music over at their house, or he'd be practicing. There was one Spanish number that I'd ask him to play, "La Bamba."

I didn't mind it when Jimmy began playing in groups because I never did frown on rock and roll. I didn't frown on any music, although I knew of religious Holy Roller types who were against anything that wasn't a hymn. They didn't want to hear jazz or anything too

= The Rocking Kings =

THE ROCKING KINGS AT WASHINGTON HALL, FEBRUARY 20, 1960.

cheerful. But music is music to me.

I didn't keep up with what Jimmy was doing with all of his early musical associates, but I know he joined the Rocking Kings. This was a typical, ordinary, real young teenager band. I saw them play, and they made good music. They played songs that were out around then, like "Yakety Yak," "Do You Wanna Dance," "At the Hop," "Peter Gunn," "Poison Ivy," "Charlie Brown," and "Let the Good Times Roll." I have a photo of the Rocking Kings playing at Washington Hall on February 20, 1960, with Lester Excano on drums, Webb

Lafton and Walter Harris on saxes, and Robert Green on piano. Jimmy's playing his white electric guitar.

The Rocking Kings played at the Birdland, a place over on 22nd and Madison Street. It used to be a theater, and then they made it into a club. It was just across the street from Honeysuckle's Pool Hall. The club was for teenagers, and they didn't sell any hard liquor, only pop. It was a place where the kids would pay to go in and dance. In later years they tore down the Birdland, and now it's a parking lot.

I don't know if the Rocking Kings played for

JIMMY PLAYING WITH JAMES THOMAS & HIS TOMCATS, 1960. THAT'S JAMES THOMAS AT THE MIKE.

any weddings, but they did play for picnics and parties. Jimmy did Chuck Berry's duckwalk and put his whole body into it while they were performing, but he didn't show off while he was in the Rocking Kings. None of them seemed like a showboat to me.

Pretty soon Jimmy started telling me about this guy James Thomas, who had drums and all kinds of instruments in his home. James was a grown man, but he wasn't as old as me. He lived in the Central Area and had a family. He had a regular job, but he was always into music. He'd get the kids together—ten or fifteen of them—and they'd all play instruments.

James Thomas was always searching around trying to find music deals. He would organize different groups to go play for weddings, parties, and picnics, and he also got gigs for

the guys at army bases. James called his whole entourage James Thomas & His Tomcats, so he considered all the guys his Tomcats, and James would more or less act as their manager. He'd say, "We're all gonna get paid fifteen dollars apiece," but it was very seldom anything like that happened. The guys in the band would always end up with a zero, or maybe even owing James something.

One time Jimmy left me a note saying that he and some of the group had gone to play in Vancouver. Walter Harris told me that the car broke down, and they ended up having to push it. After a whole lot of problems, Jimmy just said, "Man, I'm so disgusted, I ain't gonna play with those guys no more." But each time a chance to play came around, he just couldn't turn it down. He'd say, "Well, maybe this time's gonna be better." Jimmy had all kinds of hassles, but he always went back for more.

Sometimes the group just couldn't get together and play without one of the guys saying, "You're supposed to do this, you're supposed to do that." The musicians would get to arguing amongst themselves, and Jimmy told me that he'd tell them, "Yeah, yeah, yeah. I'm going out here on the porch, and you guys get yourselves together. Find out who's gonna play this riff and how we're gonna come in. When you get it together, then come and get me."

One of the places Jimmy played, the Spanish Castle, was a roadside stop down on old Highway 99 on the way to Tacoma. I've never been in the place, but they had live entertainment. Jimmy used to go out there and want to jam with some of the groups. I imagine that's where he got the song title for "Spanish Castle Magic." I don't know what the lyrics mean, though—it don't take a day to get there!

❧   ❧   ❧

FOR A WHILE Jimmy came home without his guitar. I'd ask him where it was, because he always had his guitar with him. He told me that he left it over at James Thomas' place. I said, "I always told you to bring your things home. You don't leave them around."

"It will be all right over there."

I got a little mad, and I finally had to say, "You bring it on home. Tomorrow you go over there and get it. And don't be leaving it nowhere else, because you don't know who comes in and out."

Finally he told me his guitar had been stolen during an intermission at the Birdland. I got mad because he'd lied about it, but he was afraid I'd blow up if he told me it got stolen. I said, "I guess you're just going to have to wait to get another one."

For a few days Jimmy was going around with nothing to do, his hands in his pockets, missing the guitar. Then he went over to my brother Frank's house. Mary noticed that Jimmy was down in the dumps, so she said to him, "You go down there and get another guitar at Meyers Music," which he did. I don't know how much she paid for it or if she was getting it on time, but I know he came home with a guitar.

I said, "Did you get your guitar back or something?"

Jimmy said, "Oh, no. Aunt Mary, she got this one for me."

"No way! You take it right back to Mary's or the store. You won't get one until I get you one." I just felt that if I couldn't get a guitar for Jimmy, there wasn't going to be one. I don't remember how long it took me to get him another guitar—maybe a month or so—but that second electric guitar I got him was the same one I sent to him while he was in the service.

Jimmy liked his music, and he liked playing for people. I started to have curfews for him at one time because I just wanted to know where he was at, but after that his band started play-

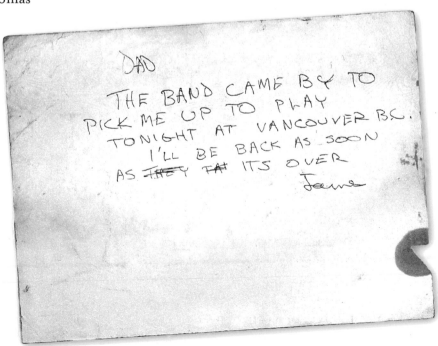

DAD
THE BAND CAME BY TO
PICK ME UP TO PLAY
TONIGHT AT VANCOUVER BC.
I'LL BE BACK AS SOON
AS ~~THEY~~ ~~FAT~~ ITS OVER
Jame

ing around at different places that didn't close until one or two in the morning, and that was understandable. I just didn't want him to be going around getting in trouble.

Usually Jimmy had two or three buddies he liked to hang around with, but at one time while we were still living on East Terrace he was getting mixed up with a gang. But the gangs back then weren't near as bad as these guys today who tote guns and do a whole lot of bad stuff. The way the gangs worked when Jimmy was a kid, if you were running around with the bunch and you didn't do the same things the rest of them were doing, they'd call you chicken.

Some little incident came about involving vandalization, and I said to Jimmy, "Now, you have no business doing this."

Jimmy said, "The other guys called me chicken! The rest of them . . ."

"Look," I told him, "you don't go blindly out and follow everybody else. Don't you have a brain of your own? If you caught somebody jumping off the roof, are you going to jump off the roof too? Don't be so stupid and do anything like vandalizing somebody's property. You don't want your property vandalized. You gotta think both ways on the thing. And another thing, about them guys calling you chicken— yeah, be chicken. Show them that you have better sense than they have. You have your own mind. Don't follow the crowd. Think it out. Just tell them, 'No, I ain't gonna do that. That's stupid. What are you doing it for?' They're doing it because somebody else told them to. It just doesn't make sense."

Then Jimmy and a friend broke into a place and stole some clothes. When I found out about it, I said to Jimmy, "What the heck! Were you going to sell the clothes?"

He said, "No, I was going to give them to the Goodwill or some needy people."

After he pulled that heist, we went and straightened it all out with the store owner. Jimmy and I went out to the guy's private home and did some work for him as restitution, but the guy still insisted on paying me for the yard work.

Jimmy started going to parties and drinking a little bit—of course, I didn't know anything about it! I did know he smoked, though, because when we lived in that old apartment on East Terrace, we had to use the bathroom down the hall. If I'd go down to the bathroom behind him, I could smell smoke, so I knew he was smoking. Finally I caught him at it one time after I'd been in the pool hall. It was on a Saturday night, and I came walking down the sidewalk and happened to look up the street and see Jimmy with one of his friends, but he didn't see me. I stepped back out of the way, and when they had almost got right up to me, I stepped out. Jimmy had a cigarette, and he just *whoop*, tossed it behind him. I had to laugh. I said, "You might as well finish that." He felt all sheepish. Jimmy did his share of gum-chewing back then too, but he wasn't a rebel.

I never argued with my folks over anything, and that's the way Jimmy was. Even as he got older, Jimmy never, ever talked back to me. He would answer back, but he wouldn't outright argue with me over a point. He'd try to tell me his side, but he'd hardly ever strongly disagree about anything. Sometimes he'd raise his voice or kind of whine about something, but he'd never do like some of these kids who yell, "The hell I will!" He never got close to arguing a point like that. It was more like, "Well, dad, it's such-and-such," in a more relaxed tone. He didn't show his anger to me all that much.

While we were living on East Terrace I was going with a girl named Esther. She wanted to get serious, but I was still cautious. Then I met Willeen Stringer. What attracted me to

WILLEEN AND ME, AUGUST '60.

Willy was her daughter, Willette. She was around three years old, and I liked her. Willeen and Willette used to come to the apartment building because they knew some people down the hall from Jimmy and I. We had the front apartment. These other people had the back apartment, and Willeen would have the woman baby-sit for her when she went out. Jimmy and I didn't have a TV, but these neighbors did. I had a phone and they didn't, and they'd want to use my phone a lot of times. So they told us to come back there and watch TV when we wanted to. So Jimmy would sometimes go back there and watch TV in the evening. I did too.

Willeen lived down the street in a rental house, and I started going down there. She was happy-go-lucky, and we were compatible, sitting there talking. She'd invite me to stay for dinner, and then she told me to have Jimmy come over to eat supper too. I didn't do any cooking up there in that place on Terrace, although we had a hot plate. I just didn't like having roaches around, so we would eat in a restaurant most of the time. Any time I'd bring leftovers, I'd stick them in the refrigerator where the roaches couldn't get at them.

Jimmy still wasn't fussy about what he ate—just bring him some food! Of course, when he ran around with his friends, they had some particular places where they'd like to go and eat. There was one place right across the street from Garfield High School that was famous for its hamburgers. There was also a barbecue place in the Central Area, the Hills Brothers. The place was nicknamed the "Dirty Brothers," because people said that if they dropped a piece of meat, they'd pick it up, brush it off, and serve it to you. But they did a rushing business, and Jimmy and his friends would get a barbecue sandwich or a meal there. But when we'd eat together, I'd go to the most economical place.

After Willeen and I started going together, we all moved in together at 2606 Yesler Way, right near 26th. Naturally Jimmy came along too. We had a house unto itself, a nicer place that's still there. It had some mice and a roach or two, but I sprayed poison all around and got rid of them. The Wilsons ran a store right across the street from us, and that's still there too.

Willeen was good to Jimmy, and Jimmy liked her and treated Willette like a little sister. Jimmy liked kids, and he'd tease and play with Willette and they'd yackety-yack. I'd go to the Wonder Bakery, where they sold day-old bread, and get them some cinnamon rolls. Sometimes I'd go out and get some ice cream, and Jimmy and Willette would love that. Willeen fixed Jimmy a lot of greens, because he liked those.

One of my gardening customers worked in a store where they sold record players, so I got a good deal on one of the first stereos that came out. It was a turntable with two detachable satellite speaker boxes. Jimmy would split the speakers apart, set one over on one side of the room and one on the other, and this would give it a stereo sound. The stereo played LPs, 45s, and 78s, and if you pushed a button the arm would swing back to a particular place on the record.

Jimmy would put my 45s on that turntable and play along on his guitar. He'd try to copy what he heard, and he'd make up stuff too. He lived on the blues around the house. I had a lot of records by B.B. King and Louis Jordan and some of the downhome guys like Muddy Waters. I liked most of the blues guitar players and Chuck Berry. Jimmy was really excited by B.B. King and Chuck Berry. He was a fan of Albert King too, because he liked all them blues guitarists. Jimmy also had some of his own 78s and 45s, but he never did ask me to buy him any records. He would buy his own. I still have some of those 45s he enjoyed playing.

We also had a radio and a television on Yesler. I didn't see Jimmy pay too much attention to the radio, but he liked to lay on the floor or sit on the couch and watch TV. Usually when I'd come home from work, he'd be sitting there with the TV on, and then he'd be playing along to the stereo during commercials. When the program would come on again, he would watch that again.

One of Jimmy's favorite TV shows was that one with Opie—*The Andy Griffith Show.* We both liked that. We'd always laugh about that beginning part where they were walking along and Opie would lose his fish and he'd run back and get it. Opie would throw a rock in the water, and Jimmy would laugh about that. One of Jimmy's favorite comedians—and mine too—was Jonathan Winters. Jimmy was crazy about him. Jonathan Winters used to set up a conversation and play the part of two or three different people. He'd do a whole lot of crazy things. He was only on TV for a half-hour or fifteen minutes, and I'd say, "Damn, I wish they'd have him on there longer." It seemed like he'd just ad-lib, and he was so comical. Jimmy and I both used to laugh, and a lot of times Jimmy would repeat Jonathan Winters' routines. Sometimes Jimmy would do funny voices, and he got that from him.

Jimmy liked them old shoot-'em-ups too. I especially liked *Gunsmoke* and *Maverick. Bonanza* was okay, but it wasn't as exciting as *Gunsmoke*, which we both enjoyed. We watched *Cheyenne* and *Wyatt Earp*—"old burpin' Earp," I called him—as well as shows like *The Untouchables* and *Dragnet.* Of course, Jimmy liked a lot of those old weird ones, like *Outer Limits* and *One Step Beyond.* He also liked *The Beverly Hillbillies* and cartoons, especially Sylvester Puddycat and Tweety Bird. And I'm sure Jimmy watched music shows like *American Bandstand.*

Jimmy started to grow his hair in different styles. I don't think he ever conked it—at least not while he was home—because he could just put pomade or Vaseline on it, fix it up high like a pompadour, and go out the door. That's the way guys were doing it at that time. They'd also wear little tight suits with peg-leg pants, narrow belts, and jackets with small lapels. Jimmy wanted to look sharp when he was playing. He wore a lot of white shirts—as many as I could get him—and a tie. I said, "Where'd you get into the white shirts?" I

Jimmy played along to records on our first stereo.

didn't have any myself, because for the work I did, I just wore something warm and comfortable. It never bothered me when Jimmy began dressing fancy, though. I just said, "If you can afford it, it's all right." Jimmy would also get all dressed up to go see some gal, but when he was just going around with his buddies, he'd dress ordinary. Jimmy wasn't overly fussy about his appearance. He didn't spend a lot of time in front of the mirror like my brother Frank, who could spend all day there.

One time Jimmy had to rent a red jacket for a show. The day that he was taking it back, he said, "Let's get a shot of you and me in this jacket before I have to return it to the rental shop." Willeen took that snapshot of him playing guitar out on the side of the house on Yesler Way.

Sometimes I'd get a report from the school board saying Jimmy had missed school, and I'd talk to him and tell him, "You better stay in school." Near the end of his time at high school, Jimmy mentioned to me about this white girl sitting right next to him, and how the teacher knew they were doing a lot of talking back and forth and holding hands. I guess the teacher was on the prejudiced side, and he made some remark to Jimmy and the girl.

That's not why Jimmy quit school, though. He was bound to quit anyhow. Jimmy's schooling got boring to him, the same way it had for me. After he dropped out, he tried to get a job as a busboy or as a bagger or box boy in some of the supermarkets, but he couldn't get a job of that sort. They didn't say it was because he was black, but they didn't have blacks doing that work in the days before civil rights. They didn't even have black cashiers, except at the Wonder Bakery.

So I said, "Well, you can come help me, since it's all for the cause—the family." So Jimmy went to work for me for several months doing landscaping. He was a little slow at first. He didn't like messing around in the dirt and

getting his hands dirty, but after a while it didn't bother him. He enjoyed it. He liked running the mowers, and he was a good worker. I had another helper named Shorty, and the three of us did a lot of work together.

I took Jimmy and Shorty out to Mercer Island, and we did some pretty big places there. All three of us had mowers because one family on the island had a lot of acreage. They also had a big orchard, so I pruned the trees in the winter and kept up the lawn in the summer. We would spend the whole day at their place because there was a lot of territory to cover. After he formed the Experience, Jimmy talked about wanting to get a place down near the water on Mercer Island.

Sometimes I would get extra helpers down at what we used to call "The Millionaires' Club," which was a place where transients would gather. I'd pay them by the hour. If I went down there two days in a row, I could tell which were the lazy ones. I'd tell the guys working for me, "Just keep moving along. Don't be sitting there doing nothing and having a conversation, especially when the people in the house are peeking out the curtain." It looked bad to be paying these guys by the hour if they were sitting there lollygagging. A lot of the guys didn't want to work for me because I'd push them so hard. Jimmy, though, he didn't seem to mind all the hard work. I gave Jimmy an hourly rate, but he never did ask how much he was getting paid.

In May 1961 Jimmy got picked up in a stolen car. After he was arrested, he called home and told Willeen he was in jail. I went down to the juvenile hall to find out what it was all about. They told me he was just sitting in the car with some friends. Jimmy told me that he didn't know the car was stolen. It turned out that just about the only one who knew it was stolen was the guy driving it. They held Jimmy at juvenile hall for a few days while they investigated what happened, and then he got the matter all straightened out. He didn't have to serve any time.

I was a little disgusted, but the same thing had happened to me in Vancouver when I was young. This tipsy guy let my friend Willie Dell have his car—at least that's what Dell told me. Dell drove the car over to our place, and shoot, a car ride in those days was something. You didn't get a car ride all that much. So we went riding out to Stanley Park, picked up a couple of girls that we knew, and came back. I don't know how they found Dell over at my place, but after a while the police came by. I guess the guy woke up and saw his car gone. Dell just told them, "Well, hell, the guy told me I could use the car." Anyway, the guy got his car back, and everything was all right. So I thought about that when Jimmy got in trouble.

Jimmy never had a driver's license while he was living at home. In fact, I don't think Jimmy ever had a driver's license, even though he owned three Jaguars after he began playing with the Experience. Jimmy needed glasses for seeing distances and for driving. A friend once told me that when you got in the car when Jimmy was driving, you were taking your life in your hands. But I never did see him drive, because after he came home as the Experience, I just drove him around wherever he wanted to go.

The same month he got in trouble with the stolen car, Jimmy enlisted in the U.S. Army, but that didn't have anything to do with his getting arrested, like some have written. Jimmy was classified 1-A by the draft board, which meant he could have to go in and serve at any time. He started seeing a sergeant at the recruiting office, and he decided to join the Screaming Eagles. He may have seen the Screaming Eagle patch in a book or somewhere, and he wanted to get one of them. The enlisting sergeant told him, "In order for you to get that patch, you have to enlist in the 101st Airborne, and that's the paratroopers. If you wait until you're drafted, you're just thrown into a pool, and you have no choice of what part of the service you go into. But if you volunteer, you make your own choice."

Jimmy told me that he had been talking to an enlistment sergeant. I felt good when he said, "I want to get one of those Screaming Eagle patches."

I said, "You sure must want it awful bad. You're going to be doing more than I ever thought of doing, jumping out of them planes." When he was younger and asked me about what I did during the war, I'd told Jimmy about seeing those paratroopers at Fort Benning, and maybe that figured into his decision too.

Just before he went in the service, Jimmy told me that he was going to make it in music. This happened after we got through working one Friday afternoon, and my brother Frank was there too. We were in the kitchen, and Frank and I were having a drink and carousing around.

Jimmy was saying, "Yeah, dad, I'm gonna be famous one of these days."

"Hurry up," I told him. "I'm getting tired of working!"

I always thought Jimmy was going to make it, but I thought maybe he would make it in one of these cabaret-type acts that go around city to city playing in the clubs. I didn't ever imagine he'd become a big rock star with world renown. I felt that following the same trend of music that everybody else was doing is a hard trail, so I told him, "When you get into the music business, do something original. And if you do come out with something extraordinary, people will take note: 'Hey, there's something different.'"

And that's sure what he did. After Jimmy became famous, I remembered that conversation and thought to myself, "Yeah!" ❧

JIMMY VOLUNTEERED for the 101st Airborne and went in the service in May 1961. Other than living in Berkeley when he was small and that one trip to Kansas with Mrs. Jeter, Jimmy had never been out of Washington or British Columbia before. He'd never been on an airplane either.

First he was sent to Fort Ord, California. Not long after Jimmy went in, the army sent me a letter saying that he had become a sharpshooter, and I don't think Jimmy ever even shot a gun before that. He never went hunting, and I didn't have any guns—and if I

To Dad and Mom
From James with love
always 30ᵗʰ June 1961

TAKEN: JUNE 20ᵗʰ 1961

did, I sure wouldn't have let him shoot them! But they used to do the same thing when I was in the Army—send the news back home to your folks whenever you passed different classes.

Jimmy wrote me several letters while he was in the army. I looked forward to getting them, because I knew how it is when you get in the service: You feel like writing every day just so you can get some mail back. When everybody else gets mail but you, you feel bad.

On June 8, 1961, Jimmy sent me his first letter from Fort Ord. "Well," he said, "I know it's about time for me to write. We had a lot of things to do down here, though. How's everybody up there? Fine, I really hope. The weather here is pretty nice except that it's pretty windy at times because the ocean is only about a mile away. I can't say too much because we have to clean the barrack up a little before we go to bed. I just wanted to let you know that I'm still alive, although not by very much.

"Oh, the army's not too bad so far. It's so-so although it does have its 'ups and downs' at times. All, I mean all my hair's cut off and I have to shave. I only shaved two times so far counting tonight since I've been here. I won't be able to see you until about 2 months from now—that's if I'm lucky. We're going through Basic Training—that's the reason. Although I've been here for about a week, it seems like about a month. Time passes pretty slow, even though we do have a lot to do.

"How's the gardening business? I hope it's doing fine."

Jimmy went on to say that the army was a lot more expensive on the soldiers than when I was serving. During World War II, we didn't have to pay for anything—it was all GI issue. But when Jimmy went in, they had to pay for certain things, like their boots. They also had to pay income tax, and we didn't. In that same letter, Jimmy said that he thought it was more expensive being in the army than it was living as a civilian. He mentioned that he had to buy

his laundry bag, hat, locks, towels, shoe polish, razor blades, and even his insignias and haircut. They'd only given him five dollars when he went in, and he'd already spent more than ten. He wasn't getting paid again until the end of the month, so he wanted me to send him five or six dollars as soon as I could.

Jimmy addressed the letter to "Mr. + Mrs. James A. Hendrix" because at the time he went in, I had planned on marrying Willeen, but then she goofed up and stayed out all one night. After that I said, "Damn, I don't want to go through this crap again—fooling around and all that. That's it." She just did it the one time, but that was that. Willeen and I broke up.

Later that month, Jimmy sent me his army portrait. In August, he sent a letter from Fort Ord that reminded me of what it was like when I got to Fort Benning: "Everything's same as usual, except we hardly do anything now. The Company left last Saturday morning at 0800 and everybody except 4 of us are gone home. The silly reason us 4 are still here is that we're still waiting for our orders to come in. They told us what we get and where we're supposed to be going. I'm supposed to be going to Ft. Lee, Virginia at a clerical and typing school. They might just change that when my official orders come in." He also mentioned that he'd qualified as a sharpshooter with an M-1, and that he wanted to send his love to Betty Jean.

Jimmy and Betty Jean had been corresponding, and then when he came home on furlough that fall, she came over and visited. Jimmy felt good about being clean-cut, and he wore his uniform most of the time when they went out. I can't remember Jimmy playing any music while he was home. He spent most of his time seeing Betty Jean and driving around with his friends. I still had the truck, but he never asked to borrow it.

While Jimmy was talking about the army, I noticed he had grown up some. He said, "Yeah, it's something else. It does teach you a few things, like self-reliance." But it wasn't something that he wanted to make a career out of—it was just something that he had to do.

When Jimmy and I would get to talking about serving, I'd say, "Yeah, I notice it hasn't changed too much except for the pay."

He told me that doing that landscaping work with me was useful for him when the officers put some of the troops on detail to clean up around their quarters. Jimmy said, "Yeah, that gardening came in handy. They'd have some of us doing weeding and mowing, and some of the guys would be griping about it. But shoot, weeding was a cinch to me." He'd show the guys some of the shortcuts.

Jimmy had some problems with his teeth when he was young. He had a little space in his natural teeth, so my sister and I used to call them his "Bugs Bunny teeth." He'd just laugh it off as a joke, but then he got them fixed when he was in the service.

After Jimmy went back after his first furlough, Betty Jean came by a couple of times, wanting to fix me breakfast. She just wanted to talk with me, and she'd bring along her little brother.

Jimmy came back home on furlough at least two times, and there might've been a third time. Usually when he came home it was just him and me at the house, and he'd go and see Betty Jean and his friends.

       ❧   ❧   ❧

ONCE JIMMY set his mind on one particular thing, he had a pretty strong will, and he tried very hard to make it in the 101st. "I'll try my very best to make this AIRBORNE for the sake of our name," he wrote to me. "I'm going to try hard and will put as much effort into this as I can. I'll fix it so the whole family of Hendrix will have the right to wear the Screamin' Eagle patch of the U.S. Army Airborne (smile). Take it easy, and when you see me again, I'll be wearing the patch of proudness, I hope (smile)." He sure was proud when he did make it.

That November Jimmy was transferred from Fort Ord to Fort Campbell, Kentucky, where they had a paratrooper jump school. About a week after he got there, he wrote: "Well, here I am, exactly where I wanted to go in the 101st Airborne. We jumped out of a 34-foot tower on the third day we were here. It was almost fun. We were the first nine of about 150 in our group. When I was walking up the stairs to the top of the tower, I was walking nice and slow, just taking it easy. There were three guys who quit when they got to the top of the tower. You can quit at any time. They took one look outside and just quit. And that got me thinking as I was walking up those steps, but I made up my mind that whatever happens, I'm not quitting on my own.

"When I got to the top, the jump master snapped these two straps onto my harness and slapped me on the butt and said right in my ear, 'Go, Go, Go!' I hesitated for a split second and the next thing I knew, I was falling. All of a sudden, when all of the slack was taken up on the line, I was snapped like a bull whip and started bouncing down the cable. While I was sliding down, I had my legs together, hands on the reserve, my chin tucked into my chest. I ran smack dab into a sand dune. Later they'll show us how to go over it by lifting our feet, of course. But my back was to it.

"Oh well, it was a new experience. There's nothing but physical training and harassment here for two weeks, then when you go to jump school, that's when you get hell! They work you to DEATH! Fussing and fighting everything you do. You have to do 10, 15 or 25 pushups. They really make the sparks fly, and half the people quit then, too. That's how they separate the men from the boys. I pray that I will make it on the men's side."

Jimmy & Joyce.
Impressions Dance
Dec.

JIMMY AND BILLY COX AT THE PINK POODLE CLUB, CLARKSVILLE, TENNESSEE.

On December 15, 1961, Jimmy took a photograph of a jump tower with two soldiers dangling from guide wires. When he sent it to me, he wrote on the back, "Here's a picture of 'Dreadful' jump school. I can laugh at it now. But then, if I laughed, I would be pushing Tennessee around all day—with my hands . . . pushups. See how that poor soul is choking half to death? That's the way it snaps you, like a whip! Your loving son, Jimmy." Jimmy also took a couple of photographs from an airplane.

THIS IS A GAL NAMED JOYCE THAT JIMMY WAS GOING WITH BEFORE HE FORMED THE EXPERIENCE. I NEVER MET HER, BUT SHE SENT THIS PICTURE TO ME.

Jimmy wrote me another letter saying he was homesick: "Oh, man, it's such a drag in here." It was the same thing I went through, and when I read his letter I remembered having the same feeling. Of course, he had a girlfriend back home, but hell, I had a wife who was pregnant. Oh, it's just an empty, lousy feeling. When I read his letters, I knew what they were all about.

Jimmy also said he wanted me to send him his guitar. He couldn't take it with him when he first went into the service because they didn't want it interfering with his training schedule. After eight weeks of basic training he could have one, so on January 17, 1962, Jimmy wrote me and said, "I hope that you will send my guitar as soon as possible. I really

Jimmy wrote on the back: "Club Del Morocco, Nashville, Tennessee, May 19th, 1963. Dad, here's a picture of our band named the King Kasuals. We're one of the two best rhythm and blues bands in Nashville. The drum player and other saxophone player can't be seen." That's Billy Cox on bass.

need it now. It's still over at Betty's house."

Once I sent Jimmy his guitar, he met a lot of musicians in the army. That's where he met Billy Cox, who played bass. When Jimmy would take a weekend leave and they'd go to town, he'd bring his guitar along and go to clubs and ask some of the guys if he could get in there and play with them. That's where he got a lot of experience.

Jimmy and Betty broke up while he was still in the service. I knew this when he came home on furlough for the last time and I mentioned to him, "Have you seen Betty Jean?"

He said to me, "Betty who?"

I knew by the tone of his voice that he didn't want to say anything more about it, so I didn't mention her again. Years later when Jimmy came home as the Experience, I asked him

about Betty Jean again. He said, "Betty Jean—who's she?" So I just left it alone. It was something that he didn't want to talk about, so I never found out who broke whose heart in that relationship.

After that Jimmy met a lot of different gals in his travels. Some wrote me and sent pictures. One of them was Joyce. They were going together in New York, but she may have been from Milwaukee. She was older than Jimmy, and she was all infatuated with him. She wrote me letters saying how much she was missing him after he left and that she was so in love with him. I never met her in person. I don't know when they broke up, but it was before Jimmy formed the Experience.

Jimmy made many successful parachute jumps, and then injured his back while jumping during the summer of 1962. After that he got his medical discharge from the service. Jimmy didn't come home to Seattle, and he didn't go to Vancouver, like some books say. He wrote to me explaining that he'd run into a lot of musicians in different places, and he was going to follow his music career. I told him, "Yeah, I know. There's nothing going on back here in Seattle in the music world. If you come back here, you'll just be sitting around idle. There's always a home here for you, but I understand your situation. You want to go out there and see what's happening.

That's the way I was. There wasn't nothing shaking at home, so I left Vancouver and came down to the States."

Jimmy wanted to go East and play the chitlin circuit, and so that's what he did. He started traveling around, usually with Billy Cox, who got out of the service a month or two after Jimmy. They put together a group right after that. I have a picture of Jimmy and Billy playing in Nashville in 1963 at a place called Club Del Morocco. Jimmy wrote on the back of it, "Dad, here's a picture of our band named the King Kasuals. We're one of the two best

THIS WAS AFTER JIMMY LEFT THE ARMY. THEY WORE PUMPS AND LITTLE TIGHT PANTS AND NARROW TIES.

they'd get arrested and put in jail. The boss at the club where they were working had to pay the charges to get them out, and afterwards he took it out of their pay. Jimmy said, "Dad, I did just what I figured you'd do. I hope I didn't do anything wrong."

"Heck, no!" I said. "I agree with you. If that had been me, I'd be doing the same thing. As a matter of fact, I participate in a lot of the civil rights activities in Seattle, even though it isn't as bad as the South. You stand up for your rights." Jimmy knew I had participated in marches.

After he became famous, Jimmy told me he donated money to the NAACP and to Rev. Martin Luther King and his Southern Christian Leadership Conference. Jimmy liked Martin Luther King, but he didn't go for Malcolm X and some of the Black Muslims who believed that blacks should do their own thing. I didn't believe in that either. Jimmy and I believed that there should be no color barrier for anybody.

Jimmy felt strongly about civil rights issues all his life. After he became famous, he was so disturbed about a war in Africa. He saw a *Life* magazine showing pictures of corpses in the middle of village streets. Jimmy said, "Oh, that's horrible. I wish I could do something about it." He kept raving about it.

rhythm and blues bands in Nashville." Jimmy also told me that he and Billy made a pact: "Whoever makes it will get in touch with the other one and see what he's doing and maybe get him to come and play in his group." Later on, that's what happened.

Jimmy was against prejudice, and he was offended by Jim Crow and the way blacks were treated in some of the places he visited as a musician. After he got out of the service, Jimmy demonstrated for civil rights down South. He told me that he and some of the guys in his band went where they had a section for the whites and a section for the blacks. They'd sit in the section for whites, and then

NCE JIMMY started playing the chitlin circuit, he always kept in touch by postcards, phone calls, or letters. He'd let me know where they were playing. He told me about cutting some records, but I don't know who he was playing with at that time. Jimmy did tell me he backed the Supremes on a record, but his name wasn't mentioned on the album. He felt pretty good about doing that, because the Supremes were so well known.

Around 1964 Jimmy started playing with the Isley Brothers, and he went on tour with them. That September he sent me a postcard saying, "Well, here I am again traveling to different places. I'm on a tour which lasts about 35 days. We're about 1/2 through it now. We've been to all the cities in the midwest, east & south." The Isley Brothers went on to Florida, where Jimmy sent me another postcard in October saying the tour would wind up in Dallas, Texas, and that his new home address was 318 Fort St., Apt. 3, Atlanta, Georgia. He also asked me to say "hi" to his grandmother in Canada and to "tell Leon to be kool and go to school."

After the Isley Brothers, Jimmy started working for Little Richard. On January 25, 1965, he sent a postcard saying that they were playing in Louisiana and that his new address was going to be in Los Angeles. A few weeks later Jimmy sent another postcard saying, "Dearest Dad, as you probably know we're in California now. Drop me a line as soon as possible. My address is 6500 Selma Ave., Hollywood Wilcox Hotel, Rm 304, Hollywood, Calif." That address didn't last too long, though, because Jimmy wrote me again on May 2nd to let me know he'd "made another drastic move" and had been in New York City about a week. "I guess we'll stay here about a month," he wrote, "playing different jobs around town here, and New Jersey." His

address that time was Room 416 at the Theresa Hotel on Seventh Avenue.

While he was playing with Little Richard, Jimmy started going by the name of Maurice James, and then later he used Jimmy James. He wasn't all that much impressed with playing with Little Richard. When Jimmy came to Seattle with the Experience, he told me that Little Richard had fired him without paying him and that Little Richard still owed him a thousand dollars. I said, "Yeah, I heard about you playing with his group. I didn't see you, but some friends saw you on TV with him." Jimmy was in the background, they told me, and he had big plumes like on the hats worn by the Buckingham Palace guards. Of course, Little Richard was down in the front of the group. But Little Richard has told me in person, "Oh, yeah, Jimmy used to upstage me. I'd be down there just doing my thing, and people were cheering and clapping. I'd find out they were all clapping for Jimmy back there."

When Jimmy told me that Little Richard fired him owing him money, I said, "Hey, Little Richard's downtown now. You ought to go down there and accost him about the thousand dollars."

Jimmy just laughed and said, "Well, shoot."

By then he'd moved to the Hotel America on 47th Street in New York City. That August, Jimmy wrote me a long letter from New York saying he wanted to make some records of his own—I never did hear any of these. He also told me he was out of work again: "I still have my guitar and amp, and as long as I have that, no fool can keep me from living. There's a few record companies I visited that I probably can record for. I think I'll start working toward that line because actually when you're playing behind other people you're still not making a big name for yourself as you would if you were working for yourself. But I went on the road with other people to get exposed to the public and see how business is taken care of. And mainly just to see what's what, and after I put a record out, there'll be a few people who know me already and who can help with the sale of the record."

His letter also mentioned that he was going to start singing: "Nowadays people don't want you to sing good. They want you to sing sloppy and have a good beat to your songs. That's what angle I'm going to shoot for. That's where the money is. So just in case about three or four months from now you might hear a record by me which sounds terrible, don't feel ashamed, just wait until the money rolls in because every day people are singing worse and worse on purpose and the public buys more and more records.

"I just want to let you know I'm still here, trying to make it. Although I don't eat every day, everything's going alright for me. It could

IN THE EARLY '60S WITH MY GMC PICKUP ON
QUEEN ANNE HILL IN SEATTLE.

be worse than this, but I'm going to keep hustling and scuffling until I get things to happening like they're supposed to for me.

"Tell everyone I said hello. Leon, Grandma, Ben, Ernie, Frank, Mary, Barbara, and so

forth. Please write soon. It's pretty lonely out here by myself. Best luck and happiness in the future. Love, your son Jimmy."

I worried about Jimmy, but he was out there getting experience, and I knew what that was all about because I went through the same thing when I first came to Seattle.

By November Jimmy was on the road again, and he sent a postcard to let me know he was in Boston. "We'll be here for about 10 days," he said. "We're actually playing in Revere. Tell 'Ernie' I'm in her home state. I'm staying up here with Joey Dee and the Starlighters. I hope everything is alright. We're right next to the ocean right across the street. Jimmy."

By January 1966, Jimmy was back in New York, and it seemed like he was still a little down on his luck. His next postcard read, "Dear Dad—Well, I'm just dropping in a few words to let you know everything's so-so here in this big raggedy city of New York. Everything's happening bad here. I hope everyone at home is alright. Tell Leon I said Hello. I'll write you a letter real soon. And will try to send a decent picture. So until then I hope you're doing alright. Tell Ben & Ernie I play the blues like they NEVER heard. Love always. Jimmy."

While all this was going on with Jimmy, I started seeing Ayako Fujita, who everyone called June. She worked in a laundry, where a lot of the girls had a hard time pronouncing her first name, so she said, "Just call me June because I was born in June."

I met June through Dolores Kurber, a girl I'd known since before the war.

At the time I was going with a girl who lived upstairs from her, and Dolores told me, "I want you to meet somebody nice that needs some good company."

I was only running around with this other girl as a pastime, so I said, "Okay."

Then Dolores told me June is Japanese.

"That don't make no difference," I told her. "I don't care. I'm prejudiced in no way, shape, or form. There's only the person."

June and I met, and we sat and yackety-yacked. And boy, after that I started going by there. June had five kids—Willie, Marsha, Linda, Donna, and Janie, who's the youngest. Janie was around three years old at the time. The other ones were all grown, but June was still having it pretty rough.

I was living on

One of my first Christmases with Janie and my new wife, June.

Yesler Way when we started going together, and then I started staying at June's place on Howe Street in the Queen Anne district. For a while I was still paying rent on my place, because I'd always told myself, "Oh, I ain't going to move in with a woman, because then they have the upper hand on me." But we were getting along so good, I moved in with her and we made plans to get married.

Our wedding was a quickie. We just went down to the courthouse, and I told her I'd do it. My brother Frank was the best man. Jimmy didn't know about it at the time, because he was traveling on the East Coast and didn't

know where I was staying.

Janie was the only one who lived with us and the only one of June's kids I adopted. It was different raising a daughter, though I'd been around young girls before, especially when I was living in Vancouver. I thought, "This is something new. I have to treat her a little easier than a boy." When Janie became an adolescent, I'd sit and talk with her a lot. I'd tell her, "Now I'm going to tell you the boy's side of things." I told her straight off how things were, that the boys would come around. She'd listen to me, and she understood. ❧

ONE DAY IN LATE September 1966, our phone rang and the operator said, "London calling." At first I was wondering who in the heck was calling me—I didn't know anybody over there. It was Jimmy, and he was all excited as he told me, "Dad, looks like I'm on my way to the big time."

He went on to say he was in England, auditioning for a bass player and a drummer. "I'm gonna call the group the Jimi Hendrix Experience," he said, "and I'm gonna have my name

spelled J-i-m-i."

I thought the group's name was strange, but I liked it. All these strange names they had around then—Vanilla Fudge and the Who and the What and the Why. I told him, "That sounds great."

Jimi also talked about how he was going to sing. "Yeah, dad," he said, "all these other guys sing, even though they ain't got no voice and they're just hollering and going on. You know I don't have no voice, but heck, I'm gonna do it too."

Jimi asked how I was doing, so I said, "I'm doing okay."

He told me he'd had a time finding out where I was living, because when he was in the service I was still living on Yesler Way. He found out where I'd moved from Benson and Ernestine, who told him, "Oh, yeah, your dad's gotten married to a Japanese woman."

Jimi was all excited for me. He said, "I hear you've moved to another place and you've gotten married again. Sounds like you're getting ready to settle down, dad."

"Yeah."

Jimi was glad June and I got married, because he'd often asked me when I was going to get married again. I'd always said, "Marriage is easy to get into and hard to get out of. It's not one of them things that you can jump in and out of."

Jimi also told me he felt so good about finally being able to do things for me financially. He said, "I'm going to buy you a home. I'm gonna buy you this and that. Whatever you need, just let me know."

"Right now we're in the process of buying a home, so that's taken care of. You just take care of yourself. The family is doing okay. I'll holler when I need something. You just keep your nose clean and stay out of trouble and take care of yourself."

I later found out that Chas Chandler, the bass player for the Animals, was the one who discovered Jimi. He took Jimi from the group that he was playing with at the Café Wha? in Greenwich Village and took him to England to build a group around him, and that was the Experience.

When Jimi first went to England, I didn't think that he was going to be that successful, but then I started getting reports on him after he started playing as the Experience. There was a notice of him in some music magazines, and then one of my stepdaughters saw a picture of Jimi with a caption that said, "The Wild Man of Borneo." When she first looked at the picture, she thought it was me for a minute. She said, "What's Al doing in London?" She looked again and said, "Ooh, that's Jimi Hendrix—'The Wild Man of Borneo' and 'The New Sensation in London.'" Jimi was on his way.

❧   ❧   ❧

JIMI DIDN'T give his first album to me directly. I got one from some hippies who lived next door. It was called *Are You Experienced*.

At that time we were living in a rooming house where you could very easily hear right through the walls. I heard this music coming from next door. I was surprised that I knew it was Jimi, because I'd never heard him sing before. I had also never heard him play as the Experience. But I told the wife, "Hey, that sounds like Jimi!"

She said, "Let me go next door and see."

She went over there and told them who we were. The people came over and brought their record. They had just bought it that day, and they were so excited over living next door to Jimi's dad. They said, "Oh, yeah! You can have

the record," and I gave them some autographs. I still have that same record the hippies gave me, but it's worn out and won't play anymore.

I told them, "Now, I never heard him play as the Experience before, and yet what I heard got my attention."

When we listened to the record, I said, "Well, I told him to do something original, and it sure is," because *Are You Experienced* was something altogether different. I'd be listening to it, and just when I'd be looking for it to go one way, it'd go another. I thought, "Dadgum! He sure has added to his music." It was something for me to get used to, because it was a phase of music I wasn't accustomed to. This was entirely different from the usual rock and roll and blues-type music we were always listening to. But it was very entertaining.

I thought his singing went along with his music. I could hear the strains in his voice, and I'd think, "He got that from his mother."

Jimi was the first rock star I ever listened to. I was working so hard it seemed like I was lost in space while all this music was going on around me. I didn't even know who the Beatles were for a long time. I'd heard people talking about the Beatles, but I didn't know if they were talking about bugs or what. The first time I ever saw them was on TV at Benson and Ernestine's place, and with all that long hair, I thought they were women. I saw them dancing around to "A Hard Day's Night" or whatever they were playing, and I said to Ernie, "Ooh, look at these gals over here."

She said, "Those aren't girls! Those are men."

I had to look again. "Hey! Those are guys?! With all that long hair?"

Ernie laughed. "Yeah, Al. Don't you know who they are? They're the Beatles."

"The Beatles! No! Damn, I've been hearing that word so much, and those are the Beatles?" Man, I was way behind the times.

People ask me all the time if I have any favorite songs on Jimi's first album, and I always say it all goes by my mood at the time. I like "Foxy Lady" and "The Wind Cries Mary." Jimi's lyrics for "The Wind Cries Mary" talked about "Somewhere a queen is weeping/ Somewhere a king has no wife." Ernestine said, "I think Jimi was singing that song about you and Lucille, Al, because he was talking about the queen and the king who had no wife." I don't know all the lyrics, but his song "Angel," which came out on another album, may also have been written for Lucille. I like Jimi's other records too, like "Voodoo Child" and "Red House." Jimi could play blues.

It didn't seem unusual to me that Jimi had an integrated band, because he'd run around with kids of all different ethnic backgrounds. I thought Jimi's drummer Mitch Mitchell and his bass player Noel Redding were good musicians.

Jimi didn't ever send me any of his records, but of course I was able to get them. And then when he came home later he brought some records with him. When I bought Jimi's second album as the Experience, *Axis: Bold as Love*, I thought its cover was way out. I said, "Jimi's into Hinduism?" But that psychedelic art was becoming popular. Some people thought of Jimi as a hippie, and I don't see anything wrong with that or with hippies. Jimi believed in peace and goodwill to each other, do unto others as you want them to do unto you, and love your fellow man.

When that hippie era first came around, I didn't get right into it. When I first saw some pictures of hippies, they looked like a bunch of bums. After a while, though, I started noticing how they carried on. They weren't going for all the glory in being rich. They just wanted to live plain and commune with each other. They said, "Hey, brother," and they believed in brotherly love and no prejudices. I said, "Hey, this is cool. I can go for that." Because that's what it's all about—just plain, ordinary living life. Don't be Mr. Highfalutin' Tootin' or think you're better than anyone else. When I saw how the hippies acted, I said, "Hey! I was born too soon."

≈   ≈   ≈

HE FIRST time I saw Jimi since his army days was in February 1968, when he came to Seattle to play at the Center Arena. I'd heard about his fame and I saw pictures of him in magazines, but I still didn't realize he was as big as he was. I just didn't get the magnitude of it.

When we met him at the airport, I was in dreamland. It was a homecoming, but now he was a rock star, and the reaction was bigger than what I anticipated. I was just going down there to see my son, yet at the same time all these other people were around. I said, "I wonder what they're here for?" They were there to get a look at Jimi. A reporter and some photographers started asking me questions. I told them I was just down there to see my son come in and that I was so glad he was coming home.

THE FIRST TIME JIMI CAME HOME IN '68 WAS THE ONLY TIME I EVER WORE THAT TIE, AND I'D SHAVED MY MUSTACHE FOR THE FIRST AND ONLY TIME. THAT'S JANIE THERE TOO.

We were standing there waiting and waiting as all the other people got off the plane. Finally Jimi came off—I think he was the last one. I watched him come in the gate, and people crowded around him.

Jimi and I just looked at each other, and I shook his hand. We were both shyish, although we'd hugged before. And then Ernestine got right in there and hugged him, and I hugged him afterwards. Photographers were snapping pictures with flashbulbs.

That was the first time Jimi had ever seen me with a tie, because I was wearing a suit with a skinny tie. That was also the first and only time Jimi ever saw me without a mustache, and he was looking at me strange. He said, "Something's missing."

As Ernestine and I were walking behind Jimi in the terminal, she noticed his jacket had a little rip in it. She said, "Oh, Jimi, you've got a tear in your jacket."

He said, "Oh, nothing to it. I've got another one—no hassle."

I thought, "Hmm," because in the past I'd have been after him about tearing his clothes. He was just so casual with it, and I just couldn't fathom that.

After I picked up Jimi at the airport, I wanted to show him the house. It seemed so exciting to him to be home now, and the house was full of people, all coming in because they found out Jimi was in town. Of course, it was on some of the billboards. Benson and Ernestine were there. So were Buck and Barbara Jenkins, a young married couple we'd known a long time. Some of Jimi's cousins and old buddies were there too. A few of my neighbors came over, and all of June's daughters were there. Jimi was so joyous over having little sisters. He was crazy about Janie. He sat there and talked with her. He said, "Wow! I got all these stepsisters!"

Jimi was really happy to be home. He kept raving, "Yeah, it's been five years. Five years, dad, five years since I been home."

I had a bottle of bourbon at the house, and naturally people were drinking. I asked Jimi if he wanted one, and he said, "Can I?" I told him yeah. He'd never drank in front of me before. He also smoked in front of me, something he'd never done except for that one time I caught him with a cigarette before he went in the army.

The way Jimi dressed had changed, but his manner hadn't. He was just older. I didn't notice any change in his ego since he became famous.

"Yeah," he told me, "I used to talk about two zeroes, money-wise, and now I talk about three zeroes."

"That's the way it goes."

"Yeah," Jimi said, "once upon a time I had a hard time getting one zero!" That was when he was playing with James Thomas.

I had joined a golf club right after Jimi went in the army, and Jimi noticed a golf trophy and a picture of me golfing. "Yeah, dad," he said. "I'll finance you and put you on the tour."

"No," I said, "you'd waste your money."

Jimi talked about the time they matched him up on a tour with the Monkees. Now, the Monkees were for little teenyboppers. Then someone made up a story about how the Daughters of the American Revolution had a big fit over it. I remember Jimi telling me that they had broken off that engagement.

Jimi mentioned that he had a contract to get a certain amount of music out, and he was working on an album he was going to call *Electric Ladyland*. He said he was working with Eddie Kramer all the time in the studio he had in New York City. I said, "Yeah, I notice when I call your apartment when it's midnight your time, whoever answers the phone says, 'Oh, yeah, Jimi's in the studio.' Man, you spend a whole lot of time there."

LEON, JIMI, JANIE, AND ME.

Jimi told me he'd sometimes stay in the studio until three o'clock in the morning. He said, "Oh, yeah, Kramer and I, we're down there working on this and that. He's good to work with." The only person that Jimi worked with that I ever heard him mention a good word about was Eddie Kramer.

Jimi had so much to talk about. He tried to explain to me about the wah-wah pedal that he and another guy were working on, and he told me about the Marshall amps. Jimi mentioned that he blew out a lot of amplifiers. He had a hard time finding an amp that would hold up under the volume he liked to play at, and he found those Marshalls to be the strongest ones. I told Jimi, "Man, this is all Greek to me when you're talking about how this and that works." He'd tell me different things about the guitar, but of course I didn't know anything about it. He owned a bunch of them, and he played Fenders all the time. He told me he was advertising them and that he got free guitars off them.

Jimi also told me about Miles Davis. He said that being musicians, they associated with each other and they hit it off. He was talking about some other musicians too, and I asked him whether he'd met the Beatles. He said that Paul McCartney was a good friend. I also asked if he'd ever met Janis Joplin, and he said that yeah, he'd met her.

Finally Jimi asked me how come I shaved off my mustache. I said, "I went and goofed up on one side, so I wanted to see what it was like without one." That was the only time I ever shaved it off. Years before I had tried to grow a beard while I was overseas, but I couldn't get anything but a little stubble. Jimi couldn't grow a beard either. He had a hard time even growing a Fu-Manchu—he'd have to pencil it in.

T HAT NIGHT Jimi played at the Center Arena. It still hadn't registered to me how big he was. I'd never been to a concert that big before, and it was overwhelming.

Before the show Jimi was backstage with his friends and all the family. My brother Frank was there. Buck and Barbara and Benson and Ernestine were there too. Some girls were trying to get in backstage, but Jimi was paying more attention to the family because he was so excited. He'd pick up his guitar and plunk on it a little bit, and then he'd set it down and we'd get to talking. Just before he went on, Jimi told me, "I'm going to be nervous tonight, dad, because this'll be the first time I've ever played as the Experience in front of you."

"Yeah." He didn't know how nervous I'd be!

We were down in the front row, right in front of Jimi. Linda, one of June's girls, had a banner made that said "Welcome Home Jimi— Love, Your Sisters." That stretched across the bottom of the stage.

Oh, man, it was great when all the people at the arena were screaming for Jimi after he came out. It just felt like a big dream. I would close my eyes and think, "I know I'm going to wake up from this," and pop—there goes the dream, and then I'd be telling everybody, "Man, I had a wonderful dream last night."

I liked everything Jimi played that night. Of course, I'd gotten used to his music from listening to his first LPs, but his songs still amazed me. I was just so surprised that he did so much writing. Seeing him onstage, I wondered, "Is this all his own music?"

I was also surprised at some of his moves. He made a half-split, and I said, "Damn!" I used

to do a lot of steps when I danced, but I'd never seen Jimi doing any dancing of that sort. I thought to myself, "Maybe he does have a little dancing ability. Well, that's showmanship. You're doing something that ordinarily you don't do." I did the same thing when I was dancing onstage, because sometimes you get carried away in the feeling. Maybe Jimi's flamboyancy just came from his getting out there, feeling good, and doing something a little different. Maybe he had to do something offbeat to overcome his butterflies and get his bid in first.

After the performance people were screaming and hollering. I kept thinking, "Damn, that's part of me up there." I didn't think it was real. I know his success was a shock to Jimi too, like a person winning the lottery. You think, "No, it can't be me," and that's the way both of us felt.

I wished Lucille could have seen Jimi play as the Experience. She'd have been ecstatic!

Jimi was spending the night downtown at what was then the biggest hotel, the Olympic on Fourth Avenue, and after the concert we all went upstairs to his room. June was there, as well as Leon and Janie. Mitch was there too, although he had his own room. Jimi was complimenting Mitch and Noel. He asked me, "What do you think of them?"

"Oh, I think they're great. All three of you guys are good."

Jimi said, "Anybody hungry? I am. Order whatever you want to eat or drink." Jimi got some filet mignon, so I tried some too. We all ordered something to eat, and Jimi wanted to put all the food on his bill.

Jimi took me aside and told me he wanted to look out for me. He said, "Just send for

JIMI HENDRIX EXPERIENCE
VANILLA FUDGE
SOFT MACHINE
EIRE APPARENT

SEATTLE CENTER COLISEUM 8:00 PM FRIDAY, SEPTEMBER 6
ADVANCE TICKETS: THE BON MARCHE AND ALL
SUBURBAN AGENCIES AND DISCOUNT RECORDS

A POSTER FOR JIMI'S HOMECOMING SHOW.

anything you need." I told him we were having trouble with June's car, and so he said he'd send some money.

Leon wasn't working at the time and he owed some people fifty dollars, so Jimi gave him the money to pay them off. Then when the guy from the hotel came in with the bill, Leon said, "Here, I'll take care of that."

The only money Leon had was what Jimi had just given him, and Jimi turned to him and said, "What you talkin' about? You ain't got no money to be paying this bill. Here you're going to try and pay for the bill, and you're going to be broke again. I gave that money to you for you."

We had a grand old time, just yackety-yacking. Jimi wanted us to stay all night, but I thought that the guys were tired from flying and doing all that playing, so I said, "No. We better get home. You guys need to get some sleep." I felt like I was imposing on him.

June wanted to stay too. Jimi said, "Yeah, it's been five years, dad. You can stay all night. We got so much catching up to do. You'll have time tomorrow, and I do a lot of sleeping on

I WAS SURE SURPRISED AT SOME OF JIMI'S MOVES!

the plane." I wish I had stayed.

The next day they gave Jimi the key to the city. He also went down to Garfield High School. I wasn't able to go that day because we'd stayed up so late at his place. Janie's sister Marsha went there with him and brought along her baby, Amanda. Jimi gave a little speech at his old high school. I don't know what was said, but it was in the paper about him being at the school.

When Jimi was getting ready to leave, June fixed him some teriyaki chicken to take on the plane. He said, "Yeah, man!" He wasn't accustomed to getting that food, and boy, he really went for it. He really ate good when he was home.

I drove Jimi back to the airport, and June and Janie came along. Before Jimi left, I told him, "Don't never get swellheaded."

Jimi said, "No, dad, I'll be the same."

Not long after that Jimi wired me money and said, "Get a new car and get a new truck too." So I got a '68 Chevrolet Malibu and a '68 GMC three-quarter-ton pickup with a V-8 engine. We got both of them on the same day. That was the first time I paid cash for any vehicle, and then to buy two at once! One for the wife and one for me.

After that, Jimi would send money any time we needed it. Sometimes I had him do that. Jimi was generous. Even when he was a teenager and didn't have too doggone much to give away, he'd share with his friends. When he was doing pretty good as the Experience, I heard about him giving away guitars.

I used the truck for my landscaping business. When they found out my connection to Jimi, a lot of my customers thought I was going to quit working. I said, "Oh, heck no." They just felt so honored. They said, "Here you're doing

JIMI'S ARRIVAL AT THE SEATTLE AIRPORT, SEPTEMBER '69.

our yard, and we should probably be doing your yard!"

❧   ❧   ❧

AS JIMI reached the height of his popularity, I just carried my life on the same as I always did. Of course, a lot of people would be saying, "Oh, there's Jimi Hendrix's dad." Or I'd be out with a friend who'd say, "Tell these people who you are."

I'd say, "I ain't going to say."

Then people would ask, "Who are you?"

"I ain't nobody. I'm just Jimi's dad, and that's as far as that goes."

I'd tell my friends, "Don't be letting it be known," but at parties a lot of times they'd whisper to other people, who'd then turn around and look. Later I'd say, "Damn, I told you not to do anything of that sort!" I wanted to be inconspicuous.

Jimi very seldom wrote any long letters once he put together the Experience. In between visits he kept in touch by phone. He'd call, or I'd call him at his apartment in New York. He'd usually ask about how everybody was. He wanted to know how my business was doing and how my health was.

I'd listen to Jimi's albums all the time, and we'd always watch him when he was on television. We were living in the Queen Anne district when we saw him on *The Ed Sullivan Show*. When he was on *The Dick Cavett Show*, we'd moved to a place we bought at

JIMI WITH JUNE'S HOMEMADE TERIYAKI CHICKEN.

7954 Seward Park Avenue.

The night before the Cavett show Jimi had been playing somewhere, and he was tired. He did a crazy guest appearance on that show. It started out with a clip of Jimi burning his guitar at the Monterey Pop Festival, which was his first big American show, and then Jimi came out. The first question Dick Cavett asked him was, "What would you say is the meaning of destruction onstage when you do it like that?"

"Hmm," Jimi answered. "I was in such a trance when I did it, but let me see if I can remember. When you watch us play and so forth, you can get it out of your system. Make it into theatrics instead of putting it on the streets, so that when you get home with your

JIMI, NOEL, AND MITCH AT THE
AIRPORT DURING THE VISIT TO
VANCOUVER.

family or girlfriend, you have all this tension out of the way. It's nothing but a release, I guess."

Then Dick Cavett asked Jimi if music has a meaning. "Oh, yeah, definitely," Jimi told him. "It's getting to be more spiritual than anything now. Pretty soon, I believe, they're going to have to rely on music to get some kind of peace of mind or satisfaction—direction, actually. More so than politics, because politics is really an ego scene. That's the way I look at it, anyway. It's like a big fat ego scene. It's the art of words, which means nothing. So therefore you have to rely on more of an earthier substance, like music or the arts, theater, acting, painting, whatever."

Dick Cavett asked Jimi about what he meant by his expression "Electric Church." Jimi told him, "That's just a belief that I have. We do use electric guitars. Everything is electrified nowadays, so therefore the belief comes through electricity to the people. That's why we play so loud. Because our music doesn't actually hit through the eardrums, like most groups do nowadays. They say, 'Well, we're gonna play loud too because they're playing loud,' and they've got this real shrill sound that's really hard. We plan for our sound to go inside the soul of the person, actually, and see if we can awaken some kind of thing in their minds, because there's so many sleeping people."

When Dick asked about what compliments he likes to hear, Jimi said he didn't like them. "I don't really live on compliments," he said. "As a matter of fact, it has a way of distracting me and a whole lot of other musicians and artists that are out there today. They hear all these compliments, and they say, 'Wow, I must have been really great,' so they get fat and satisfied, and then they get lost and they forget about the actual talent that they have, and they start looking into another world."

Dick wanted to know how you could make hundreds of thousands of dollars a year and still sing the blues. I thought Jimi's answer made a lot of sense: "Sometimes it gets to be really easy to sing the blues when you're supposedly making all this much money. It's like money is getting to be out of hand now. Musicians—especially young cats—they get a chance to make all this money, and they say, 'Wow! This is fantastic,' and like I said before, they lose themselves. They forget about the music itself. They forget about their talents. They forget about the other half of them. So therefore you can sing a whole lot of blues. The more money you make, the more blues you can sing sometimes. But the idea is to use all these hang-ups and all these different things as steps in life."

When Dick mentioned that Janis Joplin was a superstar, Jimi told him, "I'm Super Chicken—and don't you forget it!"

The clincher came when Dick asked Jimi, "Do you consider yourself a disciplined guy? Do you get up every day and work?"

Jimi said, "Oh, I try to get up every day. I'm still trying today."

When I heard that, I said, "That's Jimi! That sure is." I had to laugh, because I'd made a similar statement when I was going to junior high in Vancouver. Each kid in class was supposed to take turns being class president on Fridays. When I was supposed to be the class president for that coming Friday, I told the

teacher, "I'll try to be there Friday." The teacher laughed and said, "At least you're being honest about it."

Jimi didn't have his group with him on the Cavett show, so he played "Hear My Train A-Comin'" with the house band.

❧   ❧   ❧

JIMI CAME home to Seattle twice in '68. The second time was in September, when he went up to Vancouver and my mother saw him play. When I picked up Jimi from the Seattle airport, I dressed casual. An entourage was there, including the promoter and people with cameras, and we took a lot of photos. Some people asked for autographs, although Jimi tried to stay as inconspicuous as possible. We didn't get bothered too much.

This time Jimi checked his stuff in at the hotel where all the guys were, but then he stayed with us at our house on Seward Park Avenue. Jimi slept upstairs in the bedroom next to Janie's.

We had a house full of people all the time Jimi was there—all of his relatives, friends, guys that he'd played music with before, people who knew him from school. They'd all heard he was in town playing, and the phone was ringing like mad. Jimi sat on the sofa in the living room with all his relatives around. They were all ask-

I STILL HAVE JIMI'S OLD COUCH.

ing questions, so there was not much peace and quiet. My neighbors were excited too, peeking out at us.

One time Jimi got tired and went down to the rec room to get away from the crowd upstairs. He wanted to rest, so he napped on that old couch that we used to have on Yesler Way. I took a photo of that. I remembered how he used to sit on that couch and play along to the record player.

My neighbor next door, a mortician named Bernard Freeley, came over and wanted to get Jimi's autograph. I said, "Oh, Jimi's asleep, but I'll see what I can do." So I went down there and got his autograph for him.

We had a copy of the British version of *Electric Ladyland*—the one with the naked ladies on it—at the house. When Jimi saw it, he told us he wasn't happy with that jacket. He said it wasn't what he wanted, and that it wasn't his idea to have all the naked gals on there.

On the way to the concert, we went by the Olympic Hotel to get some of Jimi's things. Mitch and Noel went up to Vancouver in the van, and Jimi went with us. As we were getting ready to leave, Benson said he didn't have the money to go. Jimi didn't carry any money around with him, so he got seventy-five dollars for him from his road manager, Gerry Stickells, who was carrying the money. Jimi didn't have pockets in his pants, so he always carried a little war bag, just like one of those purses that women carry now. Jimi had a lot of stuff in there, but he didn't carry money. He said it was embarrassing—he couldn't even buy a bubble gum.

Jimi asked my wife if she needed anything, and June said, "I really could use a washer and

a dryer," so he gave her five hundred dollars. I imagine he was generous with other members of the family too. They probably were bugging him in the background, touching him up, but he made no mention of it to me.

Ben and Ernestine went up in their own car. Jimi, Leon, June, Janie, and I all drove up together in that Malibu Jimi had paid for. Jimi sat beside me in the front seat. My mother and Pearl, my brother Frank's first wife, were living together in Vancouver at that time, and we stayed at their place. My mom was going with Doug Shawcraft at the time. He was a Britisher, and they came to the show together.

Jimi got us good seats and backstage passes—no sweat. There wasn't any smoking allowed in the Vancouver Arena, but I didn't know it. I had on one of Jimi's African shirts—he wanted me to wear that—and I put a cigarette in my mouth. A policeman started to come up to me to say something, and then he stopped and didn't bother me. Later on I found out there was no smoking allowed. I said, "Ooh, damn. Now why didn't that guy stop me?" Shoot, I guess it was because of who I was.

Whoever gave my mom and Doug tickets placed them right in the center, just a little ways back from the stage. Somebody sent word to me that my mother wanted to see me, so I ran down there. "Al, this is too close for me," she said. "I know them guys are going to be loud!" They didn't play it like that back when she was coming along, plus there were all these people around her. So we went way up into the rafters, where it wasn't all that loud, but you could still get the sound of the music. My mother covered up her ears during part of the show. The volume wasn't a problem for me, though, because I always took something to put in my ears to smooth the notes.

My mother, who was in her eighties by then, thought Jimi's stage presentation was great, because she had been an entertainer herself. At one point mom was dancing in the aisles while

Jimi played. She said, "Let me cut the rug," and she got up and cut a couple of steps.

When he played a blues song, Jimi said something like, "My grandma and my aunt are in the audience, and they don't really like this other kind of music, so this song's for them." He also dedicated "Voodoo Child" to Pearl. During the concert Jimi banged his guitar around. I figured it was a gimmick. It was like when he burned his guitar—it left a lasting impression on the people.

His performance was certainly different than what anyone else in the family had been accustomed to, but they were all very proud of him. They said, "Yeah, he did it!" Mom enjoyed the show, of course, but she said to me, "Jimi doesn't have no voice." I also knew that Jimi didn't have a voice, and Jimi knew that himself. But I guess his voice improved by him singing a lot.

Afterwards the whole entourage went over to where Pearl and my mother lived. Pearl was a good cook, and she had all kinds of food there. Jimi and his grandmother had a long conversation sitting on the couch. They had a photo album out, and she was showing him some pictures. I was doing the rounds elsewhere, and I came back in there and said, "What are you all doing?"

My mom said, "Well, I'm just telling him things."

"Yeah, dad," Jimi said. "Grandma's schooling me. She's telling me some of the family stories." Jimi got a kick out of it, so I just left them to themselves. Jimi was very fond of Grandma. They used to sit and talk a lot when Jimi would visit her as a kid.

We sat up all night at Pearl's and left the next day. I drove Jimi back to Seattle and took him to the airport. Jimi just played that one time in Vancouver.

❧   ❧   ❧

A FEW WEEKS before he came home again in May 1969, Jimi had been busted in Toronto. I read about it in the paper. Somebody had given him some pills, which he put in his bag. Then when the Canadian Customs searched his bag, they found whatever it was, although I'm still not sure what the pills were.

When Jimi got to Seattle later that month, he checked his gear into a hotel on the North End and came and stayed at the house. He said, "I guess you heard about Toronto and all that."

"Yeah, I did. Ain't no big thing."

Jimi told me about what happened in Toronto. He told me he had said he wanted something for a headache, and these two girls gave him some pills he thought were aspirin, so he just put them in his bag, but it turned out they weren't aspirin. This whole thing could have been something his manager, Michael Jeffery, set up. I know Jimi didn't care for Jeffery.

The most common misconception about Jimi is the drugs. People enhance it like he was way out, a wild man taking drugs all the time, which he wasn't. He was just a cool cat playing his music. It's an exaggeration to connect Jimi to drug abuse. He would talk against drugs, because I asked him about them sometimes. He said, "Oh, no. I don't do all that heavy stuff. I might have smoked a little pot sometimes, but those needles and cocaine—no way!"

Then he said, "You know, dad, a long time ago when you used to take us kids to the clinic, I was always scared of the needles. I sure don't like no needles, and I ain't taking none now. I don't mess with that stuff."

Jimi did tell me that he had tried some LSD. I knew a lot of the guys were doing it. I said, "I hope you don't let that stuff overrule you." I also knew a lot of people who had smoked pot, but I didn't know what LSD was all about.

It seems to me that about ninety percent of

JIMI TALKING TO HIS COUSIN DEE DEE AND DIANE DENNISON, A FAMILY FRIEND.

the stories of Jimi's drug use were leaked to the press by Michael Jeffery. In those days people believed that the reason guys played so loud and carried on was they had to be loaded. When I asked him about it, Jimi said, "Hell, you can't play any good music and be high as a kite. It just don't make sense. Just like a drunk driver—hell, he ain't gonna go down the road straight. He's going to be all over the road!" It stands to reason.

When Jimi came home in '69, Leon was in jail, and Jimi got him bailed out. Jimi said, "Damn! Every time I come home, Leon's always in some kind of trouble."

Jimi didn't bring his guitar to the house when he came through Seattle, but he played a lot of records on the turntable downstairs. He was playing a lot of his Experience records and trying some other ones in between too. He got excited listening to his own records. He'd be telling me about when he wrote the lyrics. He told me that one time he was on the train, and as the ideas for lyrics came into his head, he wrote them down on his cuff or any little piece of paper he could find. I know Jimi didn't read any music. He knew basic music, like the scale,

but he couldn't write it note by note. That's why I wondered how he managed to write his songs.

I used to write music when I was mowing lawns. When you first get your mower sharpened, you don't want to hit any rocks. Well, of course, you're going to hit one. I used a reel-type mower most of the time instead of a rotary, and the reel makes a nice *ssssh*. But after you hit the first rock, it's *ssssh, ka-tung, ssssh, ka-tung*. It gets a rhythm to it, so I'd amuse myself with this rhythm while I'd be going back and forth mowing. I'd hum a little tune, and then I'd start jotting down what I thought the notes were. If musicians would look at it, it would seem like a lot of hen scratching and they wouldn't understand it, but I knew what it meant. I did the same thing with the saxophone. I'd be jotting down different notes that seemed to be in the scale, and I could read my music back, but nobody else would be able to read it. That's why I thought, "Maybe that's what Jimi did. Maybe he had some kind of code."

Jimi saw a saxophone I had at the house, and we reminisced about that saxophone I had gotten some years before when I got his first electric guitar.

He also asked me where his mother was buried. At that time I didn't know, but in recent years I found out she's buried in the same cemetery as Jimi. Another thing he asked me about was Mrs. Champ, the woman who lived in Berkeley. He asked if I'd ever heard from her. I said no, and Jimi said, "I wonder what she's doing?"

That night Jimi played on a revolving stage. I don't know whose idea it was to do this, but Jimi didn't care for it. They just

I THOUGHT JIMI PLAYED GREAT AT WOODSTOCK.

told him it was too late to change anything around.

That show was the first time I saw Jimi do "The Star-Spangled Banner," and it really took me by surprise. I was sitting alongside my brother Frank and his wife, Frankie. Jimi started playing that, and I said, "Ooh, man. He's going to get arrested." I started sliding down in the seat, trying to make myself look inconspicuous. I was looking around to see if any cops were coming, but everybody was just cheering. Everything went cool, and I said, "Damn!" Jimi split his pants during that show.

When he came offstage after the performance, a cordon of police surrounded him, so nobody could touch him going from the stage to the dressing room. A lot of people were crowding around, but they weren't going to let anybody get close enough to put anything in his hand or in that bag that he'd carry. He just made a dash for the exit.

After the show, Frank and I joked about that time when we were in the kitchen after Jimi and I had come in from work. Jimi was saying, "I'm going to be famous," and I said, "Hurry up! I'm getting tired of working." We were laughing about that.

Before he left Seattle the next day, Jimi told me he wanted me to travel along with him on his tours because there was so much crap going on. He was uncomfortable with the way his affairs were being handled, because he wasn't a businessman. All he wanted to do was just play his music. He wanted me to travel with him in order to have somebody he felt was trustworthy around him. I said, "I'd just be in the way."

"But I'd just like to have you along, dad."

"Yeah," I told him, "I'd like to travel along with you, but I don't think the wife would care for it too much."

Of course, I wasn't able to go. Later on Jimi called me and said, "Well, I understand, dad."

That summer Jimi played the Woodstock festival. I didn't know too much about

Woodstock beforehand, although I was keeping track of where Jimi was going because somebody at Warner Brothers had sent us a tour schedule, and I'd glance over it.

I saw the *Woodstock* movie when it came out and thought it was great. I said, "Wow! All those people all out there in the open. Man, it's fantastic. The guys way in the back have to have binoculars to see." I really enjoyed Ravi Shankar, the East Indian sitar player. When Jimi came home in 1970, I said to him, "Did you ever meet him?" Jimi said he had, so I said, "Man, I sure liked his playing. He played so fast. That was the first time I ever heard one of them sitars playing that type of music." Jimi told me he enjoyed playing Woodstock and meeting the different performers. He said he had a fine time.

At the end of the year Jimi recorded an album called *Band of Gypsys* with Buddy Miles and Billy Cox. They put that band together during a slack time after Jimi broke up the Experience, because Noel wasn't with him and Mitch wasn't around. I don't know why the Experience disbanded because I never asked Jimi about it.

HEN JIMI came to see us in July '70, he was so thin it looked like he could stand some good square meals. He talked about how he'd like to spend a few months at home without letting anybody know he was there, just so he could lay back and take it easy and eat. He also talked again about wanting to get a home down along the shoreline of Mercer Island, where he used to work with me.

Jimi made it clear that he wanted to break away from Michael Jeffery. The first time I asked him how his manager was, he just said, "Yech!" I knew right off the bat Jimi didn't want to talk about it.

Later on Jimi told me that he and his man-

ager didn't get along at all. Jeffery just pressured him too much when Jimi wanted to rest and take it easy. Jimi said, "Yeah, I want to get away from him." As a matter of fact, he was going to see his attorney, but the problem was they both had the same attorney, Henry Steingarten in New York.

Jimi had signed a five-year contract with Jeffery, and he wanted to break that contract. He didn't like the way Jeffery was handling things on his behalf. I've read that Jeffery had apparently arranged to have some people kidnap Jimi, and then Jeffery came in there like a hero to rescue him. Jimi did tell me that he'd been put in a warehouse when all that happened. He just wanted to get Jeffery out of his face, and Jimi said that he was going to start the process after they did the *Rainbow Bridge* movie in a few days.

Jimi also told me that he wanted to get into another phase of music, to get away from the psychedelic thing and do something different. He didn't know exactly what it was going to be—blues, jazz, or what—but he said he was going to be renowned like Bach and Chopin. He said he was going to make me "doubly proud" of him, and I told him, "I couldn't be any more proud."

His last concert in Seattle was outdoors at the former Sicks Stadium, where the Seattle ball team used to play. The week before Janis Joplin was the first person to play there, and it was nice and sunny that day. When Jimi played there, it rained all day. It didn't stop the crowd, though. People stood out there in their ponchos and raincoats, and some brought umbrellas.

Several stagehands rigged a tarpaulin over the stage. There were certain places where there was a little dip in the tarp, and the stagehands had to push the water off with poles. Jimi stood halfway under the tarpaulin, but he still got wet

MY SON'S LAST VISIT HOME.

because of the breeze. With all those wires around, it's a wonder he didn't get electrocuted. And he played for a long time that night too. You'd think that he'd cut it short, but he just kept on playing. Jimi did a bunch of numbers, including "The Star-Spangled Banner."

Billy Cox was playing bass in the band at that time. I liked Billy when I met him. When Jimi introduced him to me, he told me they knew each other from the service. I said, "A good friend of Jimi's is a good friend of mine," because Jimi had talked about Billy, and I knew he thought highly of him.

The band didn't sound that much different to me than the Experience had with Noel on bass. Of course, my ear might not have been all that close to the music like Jimi's was, and I enjoyed all of Jimi's concerts equally well.

Jimi didn't feel too good the next day, so when the rest of the guys left, he stayed an extra day. He just wanted to hang around. Gerry Stickells, Jimi's road manager, stayed too.

The last day he was home, Jimi talked to me about getting married, although he didn't mention a gal. I said, "This is the first time I ever heard you talk about this. If you be talking marriage talk, it's going to have to be somebody that's really in love with you, not what you got. It's real difficult in your position. You can't be sure."

Jimi said, "Oh, yeah. I know."

"I know you run into a lot of fine hens."

Jimi just said, "Oh, yeah."

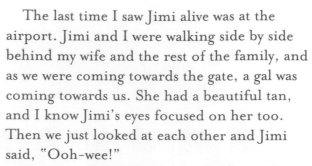

The last time I saw Jimi alive was at the airport. Jimi and I were walking side by side behind my wife and the rest of the family, and as we were coming towards the gate, a gal was coming towards us. She had a beautiful tan, and I know Jimi's eyes focused on her too. Then we just looked at each other and Jimi said, "Ooh-wee!"

As he was getting ready to board the plane, I told Jimi, "Keep your nose clean." Jimi started down the ramp one time and came back and looked into my eyes. He went down again and came back and did it again. He did that three times, and I waved at him. We were wondering if we'd ever see each other again—I know that's the way I felt, and I sensed that Jimi had the same feeling. I was always so scared every time I'd see him off at the airport, because I was afraid of the plane crashing. I felt sad driving back home that last time.

After he left, I did talk to Jimi on the phone again. He wanted the wife and me to come over to Hawaii during the shooting of *Rainbow Bridge*, just to be there and take in the sights. He said, "How would you all like to come over to Hawaii and be around while they make the movie?"

I said, "That's fine with me."

But Jeffery didn't want us to go. "Oh, no, they'd be in the way," Jeffery told Jimi, and Jimi was perturbed about that. Before we hung up Jimi told me that he just wanted to get some time to come home and be with the family. He said that he wanted us to become closer, instead of just seeing each other periodically. ❧

Jimi kisses June goodbye.

On September 18, 1970, Henry Steingarten, Jimi's lawyer, called to tell me Jimi was dead. It was in the morning, and I was still in bed. Oh, it hurt—it's still hard for me to talk about it.

At the time Steingarten didn't say how Jimi died, just that he had died in London. I can't remember if he told me any of the circumstances, because I was in shock over losing Jimi. After he hung up, I didn't call anybody

LEON ARRIVING AT JIMI'S FUNERAL.

else. I just thought, "It's going to be announced in the newspaper and on the radio and TV." Sure enough, my phone started buzzing off the hook. Everybody was saying, "I heard about Jimi dying. Is it true?"

Freddie Mae Gautier was really helpful. Right after the report of Jimi's death, she was right there at the house, taking over. Later on she did a lot of writing, answering condolence cards. I'd known Freddie Mae ever since she was a little kid when I first came to Seattle.

When Steingarten called, he told me to come to New York as soon as possible and to bring an attorney. I didn't know any at that time, so I called a friend, and she told me about Charles Pasco, who'd done some small things for her. I said, "Well, some kind of

attorney is better than none at all." Pasco went along with me to New York. This was during the few days right after Jimi's death and before the funeral, because it took several days for Jimi's body to get from England to New York and then to Seattle.

When we got to New York, Alan Douglas and his wife or girlfriend were there to meet our plane. That's the first time I met him, and I didn't know anything about him. He told me that he and Jimi were so buddy-buddy, but Jimi had never mentioned anything to me about him. He said that before Jimi got his own studio, Jimi would go to Douglas' studio to do a lot of practicing. I don't even know if Douglas had a studio, but I remembered that Jimi had told me, "Yeah, I'll be glad when I get my own studio," and that when he did, he was so happy about it.

From there on, Douglas got his bid in to control Jimi's music. Pasco and him did a lot of talking. I was busy looking out of the hotel window most of the time they were talking. I was still in shock over my son dying. That's what makes me so mad. I was so trusting with all these people, and yet at the same time I knew there was a bunch of vultures out there. Douglas was probably thinking, "This is a good time—I'm going to put my foot in the door right now and get on Hendrix's side."

I met Michael Jeffery for the first time during that trip, and I remembered what Jimi had told me about him. I also met Devon Wilson, a girl who knew Jimi. She was saying that she and Jimi were talking about getting married, but I didn't believe that. She was kind of a wild-looking, carefree hippie. She just didn't seem to be his type.

After that we went over to Jimi's place. It was hard being there and knowing that that's where he lived. Jimi's apartment was okay, but it was messy. It looked like he'd just left to go down the street to the store. He had a bunch of gold records on the wall, a reel-to-reel tape recorder, and boxes with a lot of LPs in them. There were clothes hanging up in the closet and some white buckskin boots.

I picked up a letter from my niece Gracie that was on the mantelpiece and put that in my pocket. I looked through a photo album, and that's where I got the pictures of Jimi and some of the guys taken in a nightclub in Nashville. I asked Pasco to put them in his briefcase. There was also a brick there with the Apollo logo on it, and I remembered Jimi

telling me that he had played at the Apollo and won a contest. He said that was something. He felt real good over that because it was the Apollo Theater in New York—if you weren't any good, they'd throw food at you! But later on when I got Jimi's things back, the brick wasn't there. That was the only time I ever went to his apartment.

Jimi had some sporty cars—three Jaguars, I think. He had smashed up one or two of them. They showed me one of his Jaguars in the garage and asked me what I wanted to do with it. I said, "Maybe sell it." It had been there a long time, and it didn't look like it would run. We also stopped by Jimi's Electric Lady Studio. Jimi and Jeffery were part owners, so Jeffery showed me around.

After all that I came back home for Jimi's funeral. My neighbor Bernard Freeley took care of Jimi's body. He went out to the airport and got it, and he had it on display at his funeral home in Columbia City. It was an open casket.

We had the funeral service at the Dunlop Baptist Church that Janie attended. That whole day was hard for me, naturally. I didn't talk at the service. A woman sang spirituals, and Freddie Mae read the words to Jimi's "Angel" and did a eulogy. A lot of relatives were there, including my mom and her boyfriend Doug and my brother Frank. The relatives were there too— Dolores, her sister Anne, and all of Dolores' kids—Roberta, Dee Dee, and Julia.

Miles Davis came to the funeral, but I didn't talk to him a whole lot. Noel and Mitch were there too. Johnny Winter came in, and Gerry Stickells and Michael Jeffery also attended. Jeffery did all the preparations, and he showed me a big spread he had arranged with a guitar made of flowers. The mayor of Seattle was there too.

I rode out to the cemetery with my wife and Janie. Jimi was laid to rest in Greenwood Cemetery in Renton. His gravestone says, "Forever in our hearts, James M. 'Jimi' Hendrix, 1942-1970."

My mother used to tell me that after the Irish have a wake, they do a lot of whooping and hollering and drinking. I said, "That's the way they ought to do it, instead of all that mournful stuff." After my dad's and brother's funeral, we went to somebody else's place to eat, but it was still mournful. I also remembered that Jimi had a saying, "Have a big bash when I die," and that's why we had a party after his funeral. Johnny Winter, Mitch and Noel, Miles Davis, Buddy Miles, and a bunch of other musicians hosted a bash at the Seattle Center. They had eats and drinks, and all the guys played.

A long time ago they'd say that drinking after a funeral was blasphemy. But maybe you're supposed to mourn when people come into the world and rejoice when they go out, leaving all the bad stuff behind. The way a lot of people look at it, you're going to a better place if you're going upstairs, although that depends on the way you lived. I believe in heaven. I don't know if it's the way they talk about it, that spirits are up there flying around with angels or something like that, but I do feel there's an afterlife where you'll see all your old friends and family members. I was raised that way, and Jimi was too.

Some people who were right on the threshold of death and then came back have said that the experience felt really good. Others asked them, "Who did you see? Did you see some of your relatives?" And some of them said they did. They also said that up there they don't care about worldly possessions and niceties. They just talk about how everything is so serene and peaceful—no worries, no aches or pains. You just feel good. I like to believe that that's where Jimi is.

❧   ❧   ❧

I KNOW Jimi's death was accidental. Some people said he committed suicide—that's bull! And it wasn't an overdose of drugs. Monika Dannemann, this girl he was staying with the night he died, said that she had given him some German sleeping pills, and Jimi thought they were U.S. sleeping pills. He had probably taken too many, and there was a chemical reaction with the wine he had drank earlier that night. It fizzed up in his lungs and throat, and he drowned in his own vomit.

There's also a theory that Jimi was intentionally killed. There was also a rumor that Jimi had been allowed to die in the ambulance. Monika said that they didn't lay him down on his stomach or back. Instead, they held him up in the chair. I've never heard of anybody being in a chair in an ambulance when they're out cold, so I don't know.

I was told that after Jimi died, some people went into his apartment and ripped off a bunch of stuff. While I was in New York, Steingarten had asked me what I wanted him to do with Jimi's stuff, and I said, "Send me all of Jimi's things." Michael Jeffery sent some stuff, but it wasn't nearly as much as what I saw in his apartment. I never got his jewelry or some of the other things I'd seen.

I got three of Jimi's guitars, including a twelve-string and the left-handed Fender bass. One of Jimi's amplifiers was sent along too.

They did send Jimi's gold records to me, but then they got stolen around 1985 from the house I still live in today. These were given to Jimi for the albums that came out during his lifetime. Over the years some of these stolen gold records have supposedly turned up, but they weren't the original ones, which had a brown framework and a cloth background. The ones Jimi had didn't have the little cassette tapes in them either.

There was one guy who treated me right. I forget his name, but he was Buddy Miles' manager at one time. He came forward after Jimi died and gave me some money Jimi had loaned him. "You sure are an honest guy," I said. "Jimi ain't never said anything to me about you." I thought that was really great, because I didn't know a thing about it. He was about the only one who was like that.

No one else has ever come forward with anything belonging to Jimi, although people have asked if they could buy Jimi's things from me, and I always say, "Hell, no." One time I did donate Jimi's Hopi jacket and about five other items of his to a charity auction for Planned Parenthood, so they're gone now. I wrote a letter to go along with the items, saying they were authentic, which I knew they were. Occasionally people still send me a picture of some article somebody is trying to sell to them, and they ask me if that item was Jimi's. Heck, I can't tell by a photo.

People have ripped off so many of Jimi's things, and now they're showing up in auctions. Whenever these big auction houses sell off some of his stuff, someone always asks me, "Don't you get some of that?"

"Hell, no. Whoever had it, they're the ones who get the money off of it."

Then they say, "That's not fair."

"They know it, and I know it. But there's nothing I can do about it."

This one guy who stole from me started out as a friend. He told me he collected Jimi memorabilia, and he gave me an LP that he'd gotten in Germany. Then he started coming over to visit me. He'd take pictures of some of Jimi's letters and other samples of Jimi's writing, like his hotel notes. I think he stole some of them too. I know he took a picture of Jimi and me. It was on the bookshelf in my living room on the day he came to visit me. I went to the bathroom while he was looking around, and then the next day I noticed the photo was gone. I called him as soon as he got home, and he said, "Oh, no, I didn't get the picture."

"But you and I were the only ones here, and the picture was here before, and now it's gone." Of course he denied it. Later I learned that he was selling copies of this photo. He might also be the one who got the gold records from my house.

I don't have any of the original letters or postcards Jimi sent me, either. I wanted to show them in this book, but they've all been ripped off or held up in litigation. I was encouraged to turn some of them over to my lawyers at the time for safekeeping, and that's the last I've seen of those. I tell them the letters and cards weren't returned, and they tell me they were, so I'm still trying to track down the originals. I want them back. I guess people want anything original like that as a collector's item or just to resell it. But anything that belonged to Jimi—and that he didn't give away himself—has no business being in someone else's possession. Some people just don't have scruples or feelings or passion—that's why the jails are so filled up.

I cherish all of Jimi's possessions, but seeing any of his personal things always hurts. I still have the old couch that Jimi used when we lived on Yesler Way. It was secondhand when I bought it a long time ago from the Goodwill. I kept a few other things too, like the poems and little ditties Jimi wrote when he was a teenager and a few cartoons he made while practicing his hand at making characters.

I've never parted with any of Jimi's artwork. When he was still living at home, Jimi put his drawings in the closet, and I didn't disturb them other than to look at them from time to time. Then after he went in the army, I'd take them along with me whenever I moved. After Jimi formed the Experience, I told him that I

had some of his old drawings, like the cartoon sketch of his cousin Gracie, and we laughed about that. I said, "Yeah, you were good at drawing." Then after Jimi died, I just boxed his drawings up and thought I'd keep them.

❧   ❧   ❧

PEOPLE HAVE wondered if Jimi had any children. I don't believe he did. I asked him about it the last time he was in Seattle, and he told me he didn't. I told him at the time, "Don't be ashamed to tell me—there's nothing to it."

Jimi said, "Not that I know of. I don't have any kids." So that's about it on that subject. As for that girl in Sweden claiming that Jimi sired her son, I go by what Jimi told me.

I also wasn't aware that Jimi was engaged to Monika Dannemann, as she said in her book. He didn't tell me about it. I did hear about a ring that he'd given Betty Jean, but that's the only one I know of him ever giving anybody.

A documentary about Jimi came out not too long after he passed away. It was called *A Film About Jimi Hendrix*, but it wasn't exactly what I had thought it would be from what they were telling me in advance. It didn't show too much about who Jimi was. It was more about the way he'd carry on onstage. There was nothing mentioned about his childhood days. It was showmanship and sensationalism. It wasn't real.

The record company wanted to put out more of Jimi's music. They were wondering who to get to produce the albums, and I said, "Well, if Douglas is who he says he is and if Jimi worked with him . . ." But Jimi had told me so many positive things about Eddie Kramer, and I wish I had thought about Kramer then. My new lawyer at the time, Leo

Branton, hired Douglas to do the production of Jimi's records.

For a while I had a lot of Jimi's tapes that had been found—around seventy-five boxes, maybe more. I kept them at the house for several years, and after a while Leo said Douglas wanted to do some new mixing with the tapes. This was around the time *The Essential Jimi Hendrix* was issued. Douglas came to my house three different times to get tapes, and then finally he took the remainder of them.

When Douglas produced *Crash Landing* and *Midnight Lightning* in the early 1970s, I got a lot of complaints from fans, so I guess he didn't do such a great job. He erased Jimi's original musicians off some of the tapes and dubbed in new guys. To me, that's like getting a famous artist like Picasso to paint you a picture. Something happens to him part of the way through it, so then you get someone else to try to finish up the work the way they thought Picasso was going to do it. You're going to see a borderline where the new guy came in. That's the same way it was with getting other musicians to finish up some of Jimi's music. They didn't know exactly how Jimi was going to do it, and that's all there is to it.

I didn't keep up with all of Jimi's records that came out after his death, but a lot of fans asked me, "What do you think about Douglas' way of doing the records?"

I'd say, "I guess the guy is trying to do the best he can with what he's got. Of course, it's never going to be like what Jimi did because nobody knows what Jimi was going to do."

All along the way, even before the litigation, I wasn't fully satisfied with what Alan Douglas was doing with the music. A lot of the stuff he came out with wasn't new. He told me he was putting a different sound to it, but when I played it, it was just the same. One time he told me about how he was going to put out a box set called *The Experience Collection*. It would make a person think he'd be getting something

J IMI ENJOYED BEING WITH JANIE.

different, but it wasn't. It was the same music, only packaged another way. I thought, "What the hell! A lot of fans are going to be disappointed with this. Ain't no different than the old thing." But I never said anything to him about it.

I still worked all through the 1970s, doing the same gardening and yard work I was doing before. I cut down on my customers, though, to about five places a day. I was mowing lawns, trimming shrubs and hedges, weeding flower beds. Then I quit my regular business when I had to get a new valve for my heart around 1979.

At first I didn't know I had heart problems. I just felt lousy. The doctors said that I had the flu and put me in the Veterans Hospital. I was in there two or three days, and then they let me go home. While I was laying down I felt okay, but when I got up I got all dizzified and felt like I had no energy. So I went back in the Veterans Hospital again, and they found out that I had a leaky valve, so my heart wasn't pumping enough blood to give me go-power. They told me I had to have an emergency operation. The doctor said, "When would you like to have it done?"

I said, "Do it now, or tomorrow. Just get it over with." I figure that when you have to have something done, don't be dragging your feet fooling around with it. Go on and get it done.

Leo Branton heard about me going in the hospital, and he wanted me to come down to Los Angeles, where they're supposed to have some good heart doctors. I said, "Oh, they've got some good ones right here in Seattle. Besides, I want to be close by the family." They put a permanent valve in my heart, and eventually they had to put in a pacemaker.

While all this was going on, Doug Shawcraft died, so June and I had my mom come down to Seattle to live with us. Then my sister Pat died. Her daughter called me about it, and I was so surprised. Pat had been cleaning the house and had a stroke. Gracie found her laying on the kitchen floor where she'd been sweeping. Her hair had all turned white from the stroke.

My mom stayed with us until 1984, and then she got sick and went to the hospital. I told the wife, "When mom gets out of the hospital, she's going to go right back to Vancouver." Which she did, and she stayed with Pearl until she passed away in July 1985.

Not long after my mother died, my wife June had a stroke that seemed to affect her mind. We were both retired, and after the stroke she'd sit there and watch TV and do a lot of crocheting and say things like, "Why don't you get out of here and go to the golf course or go over to Frank's?" Things got to be all hectic, and then she started saying, "I'm going to have to get away from you," which was hard to live with. Finally we separated.

We'd been married twenty years, and I was used to coming home to her. She was a good wife when it came to meals and all that, although she didn't have to clean the house because I had somebody doing that. June and I are still married and we're still friends. We don't live together, but I take care of her financially.

To a certain extent I enjoy living by myself, because I don't have to answer to anybody and

My mom shooting pool in '82.

I can do my own thing.

After I lost my mom, my brother Frank passed away from cancer. He might have been sick for a long time, because one of Frank's problems was he wouldn't see doctors. He'd get an appointment, but then when the time came he wouldn't show up and they'd have to call him. He just wouldn't co-operate with the doctors. His son Bobby asked me, "Gee, why was dad like that?"

All I could say was, "Frank was kind of strange in a lot of respects." Frank was cremated, and his ashes are in the mausoleum at the same cemetery where Jimi's buried.

❧ ❧ ❧

I DON'T KNOW what was tougher—going through World War II or battling for Jimi's legacy. They were both so bad. Winning the legacy was more of a headache.

When I made the original deal for Jimi's music right after he died, my lawyer, Leo Branton, told me, "Al, you're a millionaire." I never did ask him how many millions I had, although I wish I had at that time. The money was supposed to be in some trust that he had for me elsewhere, and I was to be paid a yearly stipend of $50,000. The checks came from Leo Branton, who told me the money was coming from a South American music company. They'd send the money to him, and he in turn would send it to me. I never got any checks directly from Jimi's label, Warner Brothers, or from anyone else besides Leo.

Despite the money Leo sent, I didn't feel relief or feel any different. I knew a lot of people would say, "$50,000 a year! Damn, with all that money, I'd be doing . . ." But I came up during the Depression days. I was going to make the most of it, and I didn't feel like that wasn't enough money. As long as I can keep the wolves away from the door, as my mother

would say. You just need to keep a roof over your head and food on the table and pay your bills and live comfortably. I never felt wealthy. I knew I had money, though, because I could buy things easier than I could a long time ago.

I assumed all along I was getting royalties on the albums that were coming out, but I didn't know how it was set up. I thought the royalties were being paid to some account that I owned.

The battle to get back Jimi's legacy didn't begin until around 1992, because before that I had faith in Leo Branton. Leo became my lawyer in the latter part of 1970, because I felt Pasco wasn't a good enough attorney to handle Jimi's music and publishing. I'd been told by a friend who knew his brother that Leo was a good attorney for the entertainment world. He had worked for the Nat "King" Cole estate, and after he became my attorney he became Angela Davis' attorney too.

At the time I hired him, Branton didn't know Alan Douglas. Once Leo agreed to be my attorney, Douglas got in touch with him and told him that he and Jimi were real good buddies and all that malarkey. Mike Jeffery reportedly died around the same time this was happening. They say he was killed in a plane crash, but some people think he may still be hiding out. I don't know about any of that.

Over the years I had heard so many different reports about how things weren't right with Jimi's estate, but I just bypassed them. You always hear rumors. But then I heard that the estate was being sold. My niece Diane tipped me off. She said, "Gee, I read something about the rights to Jimi's music being sold. Are you selling the rights there, Unc?"

I said, "Heck, no!"

She said, "Well, there's an article in this magazine about the rights being sold to MCA."

"Nope," I said. "I'm supposed to have the rights, and ain't nobody asked me. It seems to me that if something's supposed to belong to me and it's going to be sold, I'd have to give my permission."

That's when I started getting suspicious. Before that I trusted Leo because he had told me, "I won't sell you down the river, Al. I'm going to do everything in your favor." He also said he wasn't going to make any big negotiations without my consent. "You're the head chief," Branton had told me. "You're the boss."

Although he had told me I had Jimi's legacy, I realized I didn't and that I was being ripped off right and left. So I had to fight to get back what I thought I had all along. I was really mad, and I dropped Branton after I found out how he misrepresented me.

JANIE AND ME TODAY.

In April 1993 I filed a lawsuit in federal court in Seattle charging Leo Branton, Alan Douglas, and some of their associates with twenty years of "misrepresentations, mismanagement, unjust enrichments, and self-dealing." Some of the companies Leo had transferred the money to, like Bella Godiva and Are You Experienced, were also named in the suit.

When I took on the battle for Jimi's legacy, I was fighting for Jimi and the family. It was something that belonged to me, and I wanted to have it. I said, "Boy, for twenty years they just got carried away with all the money that they were taking—all the millions—and in all that time I just got a little bit out of it."

Who got all the money? Leo got a good portion of it. I guess he invested in different things. The apartments he owned in Los Angeles were probably bought with my money. Douglas had his finger in the pie too, and they worked together. I imagine Michael Jeffery

might have had something to do with it too.

Paul Allen, one of the heads of Microsoft, loaned us some money for the litigation. He volunteered to do this, and we just shook hands on the deal. Our new attorney, Yale Lewis, said we couldn't have won back Jimi's estate without him.

When I first met him, Paul told me he wanted to build a museum in Seattle in honor of my son because he'd been a fan of Jimi all his life. That seemed all right with me. Then when the litigation came up, he said he'd give me some financial help if I needed it. I told him, "Yeah, we could stand some financial help. But this money is just going to be a loan. It ain't going to be a gimme, because I don't want anybody saying, 'Yeah, I gave you this and now I want that.' I don't want anything like that."

During the litigation, Paul Allen never came to any meetings we had, but his people came and said, "We'd like to have some concessions."

They were trying to get our word ahead of time that we were going to give them certain concessions, and here we hadn't even won Jimi's legacy back yet. But those concessions weren't part of the deal when Paul talked about the loan. I said, "Hell, no. We're not giving away any rights."

So then they said, "If we can't get certain concessions, we're going to have to discontinue the loan."

Shoot, that's just like kids saying, "Okay, if I can't be pitcher, I'm going to take my ball and bat and go home."

I just got so paranoid. I told Janie, "Some people make me so damn sick! They're nice for a while, and then they see that green stuff, those dollar bills, and their eyes and their heads are clicking like a cashier machine. They're just thinking about the money."

I get so paranoid with attorneys too. People say, "Do you have a good attorney? Get yourself a good attorney." Now how in the hell do you know a good one? My mother always said, "Yeah, those lawyers ain't nothin' but liars." I'm sure there are some good, honest ones out there, but that old green stuff just turns so many heads. I'm sure glad I'm not that way.

While the litigation was underway, my pacemaker went on the fritz while I was out shopping, and I passed out. The medics had to come in and work on me. When they put me in the hospital, a doctor told me, "Looks like we're going to have to put a defibrillator in you." A lot of people who have pacemakers have them—when your pacemaker clicks off, the defibrillator takes over and gives you jolts just like the paramedics do.

While I was in the hospital waiting for the operation, I told Janie and the rest of the family, "I don't plan on going anywhere until I get all the litigation over with, win the rights back, and get Jimi's story told in my book." I carried that defibrillator around in me for a year, and then the doctor took it out. I have so many wires and other stuff inside of me now!

Leo Branton and I saw each other face to face during some of the litigation. I wasn't speaking to him at first, and then he said, "You know, Al, we can give each other the time of day," or something like that. I said, "Oh, yeah. That's water under the bridge now."

I felt so good when I finally won back the

My brother Frank and his son Bobby.

rights to Jimi's music in an out-of-court settlement in July 1995. I'm glad it didn't have to go through a big court trial and that I got what I most wanted—the legacy. Douglas and Branton and a bunch of other defendants signed over all the rights—Jimi's music, his image and licensing, the whole kit and caboodle.

Regaining control of Jimi's legacy was one big relief. I remember somebody saying, "The fat lady has sung," but I wasn't claiming victory until everything was signed, with no more loose ends. I felt better when I saw a good portion of Jimi's tapes returned to me.

Winning back Jimi's legacy means that now we can do what we see fit with his music. We'll be able to do what so many people have always talked about, which is present Jimi's music the way he would have wanted it. I haven't listened to any of the new tapes that we've recovered, but Janie and the rest of the family are sorting through them.

Now that I've got Jimi back, I'm going to watch everything I sign! I'm going to read all between the lines, all the small print, and probably have it checked out by someone else too. Janie and her husband, Troy Wright, and Jimi's cousin Bobby have been doing all the work in that respect. That's too headachy for me. That's why I tell Janie and Bobby and Troy: "This is you guys' baby." If it had just been me, I'd have been lost.

I'm the chairman of the board of our company, Experience Hendrix, and Janie's the president. I chose Janie to run our company because I'm closer to her than anybody else. It seemed like she had the know-how and the ambition. She wanted to handle more than some of the people who did a lot of talking but didn't know anything about the business. I had to say to them, "No, it's not like that. It's just like that motivation guy on TV says: 'You've got to get up and do something to earn it.'"

Bobby Hendrix has always been a worker. When he was living in Spokane after his mother and dad got divorced, Bobby had a paper route and was always working at something. He never let any moss grow under his feet. Bob went in the service, got married, and then worked with Pay 'N' Save for fifteen years. From there he started working at Costco, where he became general merchandising manager and vice president in the main office. He left Costco in 1996 to become the vice-president of Experience Hendrix. Bobby's had a lot of experience being a manager, and he has a lot of know-how. I'm just glad he's with us now! Making it a family affair makes it feel more trustworthy.

We're really happy that the family can finally control how Jimi's music is presented. It feels like my son has finally "come home," and we intend to do right by Jimi and his fans.

❧　　❧　　❧

NOWADAYS A LOT of people say to me, "Al, I'm so glad that you got the legacy back and everything is well. You're the rightful owner, so I guess you can sit back and take it easy." But I can't. It's just starting. I've got it, and now I've got to do something with it. I can't be resting on my laurels. I've got to take care of business. I'm involved in the financial decisions, so I go in and crack the whip and attend board meetings.

In 1997 we entered into a worldwide licensing agreement with MCA Records, which is handling Jimi's record catalog. One of the first releases was *First Rays of the New Rising Sun*, which

was the last album Jimi was working on at the end of his life. We found some production notes Jimi had written about the order he wanted to do these songs in. While these tracks have come out on some of the albums Douglas did, like *The Cry of Love*, *Rainbow Bridge*, and *War Heroes*, they were never put together the way Jimi wanted them, so the new album gets that straight. Another of our releases, *South Saturn Delta*, also has some songs that had been on the albums Douglas put together, as well as some demos and alternate versions. MCA issued family-authorized versions of Jimi's first three Experience albums—*Are You Experienced*, *Axis: Bold as Love*, and *Electric Ladyland*—as well as the *Band of Gypsys* live album Jimi made with Billy Cox and Buddy Miles. We've also put out a two-disc collection of Jimi's BBC recordings made in a studio in London, which we released in June 1998.

The new versions sound better than the older CDs because we got Jimi's original engineer, Eddie Kramer, to help remaster them from the original tapes that he and Jimi made in the studio. All of the Jimi Hendrix CDs that are already out there were made from second-generation master tapes that were EQ'd for vinyl albums, so they don't have as much clarity or as good a sound.

Janie's husband Troy is really into music, so he's heading up our Hendrix Records label, which will sign and develop new acts. This label is a joint venture with MCA, and our first release is Eboni Foster's *Just What You Want*. She's a good singer. We've also started a label called Dagger Records, which will be issuing concert albums recorded by Jimi's fans. The first one, *The Jimi Hendrix Experience Live at the Oakland Coliseum*, is a two-CD set that was recorded in mono at an April '69 concert. The quality of these fan recordings isn't as good as what you'd get in a studio, but people still want to hear them.

❧　　❧　　❧

IN THE years since Jimi's death, the people I've been closest to have been my mother and Pearl, my wife June, Janie, my nephew Bobby and his sister Diane, and my sister-in-law Dolores, although I don't see her all that much.

I still see some of Jimi's friends. James Williams calls me pretty regularly, and we'll go out and have a drink. Sam Johnson's in Germany, but I hear from him. I occasionally see Walter Harris, Jimi's sax player. I bump into Willeen once in a while. Her daughter Willette's all grown up and has four kids of her own. I still see Benson once in a blue moon.

I've also talked to a few musicians who knew or admired Jimi. Bob Dylan called me a long time ago. When I spoke to him on the phone, he gave me his real name, Robert Zimmerman, and then he said, "Otherwise known as Bob Dylan." He just wanted to say hi and offer his condolences. Stevie Ray Vaughan came by and played one of Jimi's guitars at the house. That was the first time I ever got to meet him, and I went to his concert. I wish I had a tape of the music he played at the house by himself, because I enjoyed that better than his concert. As he was looking through some of my old 45s, he'd say, "Oh, yeah! I remember this." Every time Johnny Winter comes to town, he looks for me to be there at his show, so I always go to see him. He was a good friend of Jimi's. I met his brother Edgar too. Robin Trower is another one who's come by.

For a long time I hadn't heard from any of Jimi's musicians, who are scattered all over. Then my wife and I went to a fair in Nottingham, England, commemorating Jimi, and Noel Redding was there. Billy Cox was another good friend of Jimi's, and Billy's wife gave me a call one time, and I talked to Billy too. I did see Mitch, Noel, and Billy at the Rock and Roll Hall of Fame.

In 1995, the same year we won back Jimi's legacy, Janie and Troy put together the Jimi Hendrix Red House exhibit as part of the Bumbershoot Arts and Music Festival at the Seattle Center. There was a lot of Jimi's memorabilia there. They did a jam-up job on it and displayed everything really nice. I donated a lot of Jimi's clothes just for that week, and I brought down our old couch and record player. There was always a line of people wanting to get in.

"IF I DON'T MEET YOU NO MORE IN THIS WORLD..."

They had a tribute concert called the Jimi Hendrix Electric Guitar Festival. A gang of musicians that Jimi had played with came to Seattle for that—Buddy Miles, Mitch and Noel, Billy Cox. One of the Heart girls sang—I think it was Ann Wilson. George Clinton, John McLaughlin, Randy Hansen, Mike McCready from Pearl Jam, Eric Burdon, Eric Gales, Vernon Reid, Donovan, and Little Jimmy King also played at the show.

The concert was outside, with a big grandstand and people standing out in the field. Narada Michael Walden had a nice program all fixed up, and they had paratroopers from the

101st Airborne jump out of a helicopter onto a spot that was marked out. I lit a big cauldron with a guitar in it, and the fire burned up around the guitar, like an Olympics torch-lighting.

I had an ugly hat on, and when I was called to the center of the stage in front of all the people, Narada told Janie, "I've got a surprise for Al." That's when they made me king. They took off my jacket and put a robe on me. Then they took my hat off and put a crown on my head. I didn't know what to think about all this! All the people were cheering, though, and I felt exuberant. Then they sat me on a throne over on the side of the stage, where the sound was so bad! Overall, though, I was really pleased with it. Even when it started raining, most of the people stood their ground. The funny thing was, the last time Jimi played in Seattle there was a big storm too. The show ended with everybody singing "Angel."

Today there are a few memorials to Jimi in Seattle. Out at the Woodland Park Zoo there's a rock with a plaque in it commemorating Jimi. It was donated by a radio station, and a lot of people complained about them putting it in the zoo. I went out there for the dedication. There's also a bust of Jimi by Jeff Day in the library at Garfield High School. I also was there for the commemoration. There's a mural of Jimi on First Avenue on the building that used to house Meyers Music Store, where I purchased Jimi's first and second electric guitars. EMI dedicated a statue to Jimi in front of their Seattle office on Broadway. More recently, an English Heritage Blue Plaque was dedicated to Jimi in London. It's at 23 Brook Street in the Mayfair District, where Jimi is said to have shared an apartment with Kathy Etchingham. Jimi was the first rock musician ever to get one of these plaques, and Janie and I watched the dedication in 1997.

❧   ❧   ❧

BEING KNOWN as Jimi Hendrix's dad is fun and a hassle. The fun part is seeing how people are still so crazy and excited over Jimi. When they see me, they say, "Ooh! There's his dad!"

I say, "Well, I'm just his dad. Jimi was the talent."

They say, "Yeah, but you helped to bring him here." That feels good.

The hassle comes when people are bugging me too much—sometimes they get a little irritating, wanting me to come here or there. "We're having a get-together. Will you come and say a few words?" I'd like to, but I can't do all those things.

Nearly every week—at least—somebody is calling me on the phone or trying to meet me in person to do interviews. A lot of people ask me how old Jimi was when he first started playing guitar. They also ask if I got Jimi to play the guitar and taught him music. "No," I tell them, "he did that on his own. But I was glad he took up the guitar. It kept him off the street—I knew where he was—and he was interested in it. I knew he'd be good at it, because if you really enjoy doing something, you could become a master of it. And that's why I got him a guitar." Many people also want to know if Jimi played the music too loud around the house. Shoot, he never had an amplifier when he was still at home, and he never played the record player that loud because I'd just turn it back down.

I've also frequently been asked what Jimi would want others to learn from his music. I think he would just encourage them to go on and do their own thing. He'd like them to appreciate his music—the way it was and what he did with it.

Of course, a lot of guys try to exactly copy his way of playing. Some of them say, "I'm going to play with my teeth and try to get it down." I have to laugh at that. Sometimes they say, "Mr. Hendrix, I got his deal down as far as I can get.

What do you think?"

I say, "Well, you're doing okay. Of course, I always told Jimi, 'Do your own thing.'"

I've seen sheet music that's supposed to be note by note the way Jimi played it. A friend of mine played it as notated, but it sure didn't sound like the way Jimi did it! Maybe that's because Jimi was Jimi. He had so many ideas and could visualize so many things. It was like his mind was overboiling, like a pot on the stove overboils with so many ingredients.

The reason Jimi excelled so much is that he did something that he enjoyed. He expressed himself with his music. He was always experimenting with something different and trying to outdo what he already did—trying to get something more into the music. It was like he was saying, "There must be some new notes or something fantastic out there." He wanted to make music of the future.

"...I'LL MEET YOU ON THE NEXT ONE AND DON'T BE LATE."

❧   ❧   ❧

I STILL MISS Jimi. Not a day goes by that I don't think about him a good part of the day. Sometimes I've felt his presence. That's just how you feel about people who are deceased. If they were close to you, you just wonder where they're at and if their soul is around.

I visit Jimi's grave about once a month. I visit my mother's grave too. They're buried side by side. My wife and I will be buried right next to Jimi on the other side. Lucille's out there somewhere in the same cemetery, but she doesn't have a headstone. My brother Frank is there too.

I'm a realist, and it is a fact that we all have to go sometime. Young people don't want to talk about death, but then when you get older you just say, "Well, it's inevitable." It's going to happen, but you don't know when. I'm not scared of going, although I don't want to go violently or before my time.

Some say heaven and hell are here on earth, that life is life and then you're dead. I don't know, but I feel like there's something more.

I feel pretty satisfied with the way I've lived. I've had a lot of happy moments. Of course if there had been some way I could have prevented Jimi's untimely death, I would have, but there isn't too much else I would have changed.

Right after Jimi's death, I heard somebody say, "After a few years people will forget about him." But shoot, it's surprising how people still keep talking about Jimi.

When I hear Jimi's music today, it makes me feel good. I think to myself, "They're still playing it."

And if Jimi could hear it, he'd say, "Yeah! They haven't forgotten me yet!" ❧